# What people are saying about Revolutionary Agreements . . .

*Revolutionary Agreements* is a thought-provoking and inspiring set of techniques to facilitate true peace in personal relationships . . . a great book.

> —Former US Congressman Dennis J. Kucinich,
> 2003 recipient of the Gandhi Peace Award

*Revolutionary Agreements* line up like a stairway to a better life. Each step will raise your level of awareness, enabling you to see the greatness that has been placed in your marvelous mind. Read it, then internalize it. Your reward will be well worth the time and effort invested.

> —Bob Proctor, author, *You Were Born Rich*;
> master teacher, *The Secret*

*Revolutionary Agreements* is a series of powerful and profound life messages that can open up a world of possibilities for you. A great book!

> —Brian Tracy, author, *Million Dollar Habits*

*Revolutionary Agreements* is an extraordinary guide for building high-performance cultures. Marian magnificently shows readers how to be their best and bring out the best in others, which is key for any organization that adds true value to the marketplace and world. *Revolutionary Agreements* is an invaluable sourcebook for honest, fulfilling relationships in the workplace and beyond.

> —TC North, PhD, high-performance coach and speaker;
> coauthor, *Fearless Leaders: Sharpen Your Focus: How the New Science of Mindfulness Can Help You Reclaim Your Confidence*

Marian Head is a true student of Tao. Her insightful and persuasive "Wu-Wei" approaches for personal transformation reach our hearts with open invitation to join the "soft" revolution and harmonious agreement for all.

—Chungliang Al Huang, president and founder, Living Tao
Foundation; coauthor, *Tao: The Watercourse Way*

I have used the Agreements with CEOs, church committees, teachers, social workers, students, and government workers to build community and improve self-esteem. *Revolutionary Agreements* is a new manifesto for the coming of the Age of Peace, Love, and Compassion.

—Reverend Judith Elia, minister, Unity of Oroville

What's so "revolutionary" about *Revolutionary Agreements* is its head-heart connection. It is a profound collection of practical things to do to be all we desire, dream, and deserve.

—John Milton Fogg, author,
*The Greatest Networker in the World*

This book is a true work of beauty in its simplicity and authenticity; it is a manifesto of hope for transforming our daily lives—and our global future.

—Josephine Gross, PhD, Networking Times Review

*Revolutionary Agreements* is brilliantly written, very moving and important. This is what the world desperately needs as we attempt to find sanity and create community during these challenging times.

—Marion Culhane, social entrepreneur, coach,
trainer, Global Family cofounder

*Revolutionary Agreements* is simple and direct. It reads easily, from the heart, and rings true. This is the instruction book many people are hungry for. Such a gift it will become for millions.

—Gale Arnold, president, Radio Tierra

John Lennon dared us to "imagine." Marian Head took him seriously and did something about it: she wrote *Revolutionary Agreements* . . . the ultimate handbook for change, a powerful template for changing the way we relate to one another.

—Chris Gross, CEO, Gabriel Media Group

The Revolutionary Agreements have changed lives, transformed businesses, and improved communities . . . It is an idea whose time has come.

—Ward Flynn, author, *The Truth Zone: Building the Truthful Organization from the Bottom Up!*

Marian Head's vision and organizational brilliance made it possible to manifest the historic Soviet-American Citizens' Summits that Soviet and Russian officials have hailed as turning points in ending Cold War stereotypes. The Revolutionary Agreements played a central role in building relationships and strengthening communication among my team members during these momentous events. Thank you, Marian: the work you're doing brings hope to the world.

—Rama Vernon, president, Center for International Dialogue; cofounder, Yoga Journal

If you're serious about personal growth, you're going to love *Revolutionary Agreements*. Study them, experience them, and watch your life change. I highly recommend it.

—Larry Wilson, founder, Wilson Learning; coauthor, *Play to Win: Choosing Growth Over Fear in Work and Life*

The gift of twelve wonderful tools called the Revolutionary Agreements has helped me to reassert my life plan, mission, and goals for my physical well-being, work, and life.

—Max Lafser, vice president, Center for International Dialogue

*Revolutionary Agreements* brings our minds, hearts, and relationships to full attention. Tune into Marian Head's strategies, and your human instrument will sing a clearer and stronger song with the world. Read and resonate!

—Don Campbell, musician, lecturer, author, *The Mozart Effect*

*Revolutionary Agreements* is a deceptively simple and incredibly powerful guide to living a richer, deeper, and more satisfying life. Having lived and worked with these Agreements for nearly 30 years, I know that incorporating any one of these Agreements into your life leads to tremendous growth.

—Laurie Weiss, PhD, author, *99 Things Women Wish They Knew Before Saying 'I Do'*

It's clean, it's fresh, and it has no pretense. Marian Head shares a simple, straightforward, powerful message that is applicable in everyday practical living—and she shares it straight from her heart to the reader's heart. To borrow from Walt Whitman, "This is not just a book. Who touches this, touches a person."

—Nick Gordon, international speaker, life coach

Marian Head has beautifully accomplished what so many have tried to do—she brings action to the adage "if you change your thinking, you can change your life." More than a book, the simple yet exquisite logic of *Revolutionary Agreements* can and will change your experience of life for the better.

—Reverend James J. Mellon, founding pastor, Global Truth Center; author, *Mental Muscle: 16 Weeks of Spiritual Boot Camp*

# REVOLUTIONARY AGREEMENTS

TRUTH

ACCEPTANCE

GRATITUDE

## MARIAN HEAD

First Edition (Hardcover), March 2005
First and Revised PDF e-book Editions, 2004 and 2007
First Kindle, iBook, and Nook Editions 2011

Second Edition (Paperback), January 2016

Original Cover Design by Gregg Lauer, www.lauercreative.com

Cover and Interior Layout by Nick Zelinger, www.nzgraphics.com

Editing by Stacey Stern, www.staceystern.com

Printed in the United States of America

ISBN  978-0-9839209-9-1
Library of Congress Control Number:  2015911743

Boulder, Colorado
www.marlinpress.com

To Peace within us all,
that we may know
Peace on Earth.

# Revolutionary

Causing or relating to a great or
complete change.*

# Evolution

A process of gradual and relatively peaceful
social, political, and economic advance.
Growth. Unfolding.*

# Agreement

Harmony of opinion, action, or character. *

* From *Merriam-Webster's Collegiate® Dictionary*, Eleventh Edition

# $\mathcal{C}$ONTENTS

# $\mathscr{I}$NVITATION

The world works by agreements, whether spoken or unspoken, conscious or not. We all have agreements—with our friends, coworkers, spouses, siblings, parents, children, and even with people we don't know. Perhaps most importantly, we have agreements with ourselves.

In 1985, my husband, Glenn, and I consciously began using a specific set of Agreements to guide our daily actions. Since then I've changed, and my world seems to have changed as well. As unnecessary drama in my life gave way to greater inner peace, the world became a more loving place.

Has the world truly changed—or is it simply that, like the caterpillar turned butterfly, I now have a different perspective? I cannot say for sure. Either way, since adopting these Agreements, I have created a more satisfying life and replaced unwanted stress, struggle, and drama with greater emotional freedom, joy, and inner peace.

From the very depths of my heart, I invite you to adopt these Agreements as your own and join me in this Revolution—and in so doing, create greater peace in your life and our world.

*You must be the change you wish to see in the world.*
—Mahatma Gandhi

Marian Head
Kapaa, Kauai

# ℱOREWORD

It is a joy for me to write this foreword for my dear friend, Marian Head. When I first met her and her husband, Glenn, in 1985, I immediately recognized their authenticity, integrity, and conscious living. As a prototypical cocreative couple, Marian and Glenn truly "walk their talk."

I later learned that behind their exemplary behavior was their conscious use of a set of agreements they had developed with a group of friends and colleagues. It is a blessing for humanity that they have generously shared these agreements with the world throughout the past three decades—and that they continue to do so.

Within the pages of this book are a rare combination of wisdom and practical guidance. For those who desire greater peace in their own lives and in the world, *Revolutionary Agreements* will be one of your most treasured guidebooks. Marian's personal stories bring to life the immense value of practicing these Agreements. "Focus on Today" exercises help you look within and discover your best self right now, today.

My calling has always been to provide the new story of humanity—a vision of our potential for good—and effective processes that lead to a positive future for all. For as long as I've known her, Marian's calling has been to demonstrate living a positive life *today*. She has remarked to me more than once, "How can we have a positive future without a positive today?"

In *Revolutionary Agreements*, Marian lays a path for a positive today *and* a positive future. This book will benefit you whether you are a leader on the front lines of cocreating a better world or you are someone focused on having the best day you can given the complexities of your life.

Although they may appear simple at first glance, the Revolutionary Agreements hold the keys to transformation. Practicing the Agreements gently moves us from Ego to Essence. This evolves us into the deeply loving people we were designed to be by the Impulse of Creation.

In my work, I have discovered that a new kind of person is emerging at this time. I call this person "Homo universalis" or Universal Human. The Revolutionary Agreements support budding Universal Humans to achieve their full potential and contribute to birthing a new society, shifting the tide toward a positive outcome during these transformational times.

I encourage you to read and reread this book, do the practical exercises that will enhance your experience of a joyful life, and invite your friends and communities to practice the Agreements with you. You, and those with whom you share the Agreements, have the power to directly affect a positive planetary shift as you exemplify the transition to a new, more loving and peace-filled world.

Barbara Marx Hubbard

President, Foundation for Conscious Evolution; futurist; author, *Conscious Evolution: Awakening the Power of Our Social Potential.*

# ACKNOWLEDGMENTS

I am grateful to my QuantumThink® coach, Alan Collins, for helping me embody much of the new thinking that led to this second edition, and to Dianne Collins for writing the important book, *Do You QuantumThink? New Thinking That Will Rock Your World*. Yes, it did.

Deep gratitude to Reverend Rita Andriello and Reverend Patrick Feren of the Center for Spiritual Living Kauai for welcoming me to the "hot seat" during their Vision workshop. It was there I foresaw with great clarity how embodying the Revolutionary Agreements leads to Peace on Earth.

My heartfelt appreciation for those readers who shared personal experiences of using the Agreements with Linda Leary, the editor of our Revolutionary News e-newsletter. Linda has a gift for masterfully interviewing people then writing a story that honors the storyteller and inspires the reader. This edition is richer thanks to Linda and our contributors.

I am eternally grateful to my editor, Stacey Stern, for her extraordinary guidance to go deeper, clearer, and stronger with my message. Her insightful questions encouraged me to delve further into the essence of my truth. The results add tremendous value for both my readers and me.

In the first edition acknowledgments, I wrote, "I would need an entire book to thank my husband, Glenn, for all that he gives to me and to life." And so it is! Since the first edition was published, I have created just such a book. To share my gratitude—and show how I rescued our marriage after a difficult year—I wrote *Gratitude Journal for a Healthy Marriage*.

Without the first edition of *Revolutionary Agreements*, there would not be this second edition! For those who I thanked at length in the first edition, know that I am continually grateful for your contributions: Carolyn Anderson, Gale Arnold, Judith Bonfoey, Marion Culhane, Ward Flynn, Susan Gallagher, Nick Gordon, A.J. Grant, Chris and Josephine Gross, Barbara Marx Hubbard, John David Mann, David Neenan, Vivian Saccucci, Laurie Weiss, and Sandy Westin.

I remain deeply indebted to Marshall Thurber who created and delivered Money & You, the personal transformation program that inspired the Geneva Group Agreements, which later evolved into the Revolutionary Agreements.

My eternal love and gratitude go to all those who participated in Geneva Group since its inception in 1985, and especially to Carol Hoskins who sustained monthly gatherings that continued discourse on the Agreements every month for twenty years.

Above and through all else, I thank the Love that created me, inspired this book, and infuses my life with passion.

# Why This Second Edition?

I am not the same person I was ten years ago when the first edition was published. Gratefully, I have learned much in the past decade of my practice—not to mention during the thirty years I have lived with Agreements since birthing the Geneva Group Agreements in 1985. Writing this second edition gives me an opportunity to explore and share my current thinking.

Also, since the first edition was published, readers have let me know how they have applied the Agreements to enhance their relationships, boost productivity at work, and increase peace and joy in their lives. While the principles behind the Revolutionary Agreements are timeless, their power lies in practicing them. You'll find readers' personal stories that initially appeared in the Revolutionary News e-newsletter scattered throughout this book in their own special format.[1]

Perhaps the most important reason for this second edition is that **these times call for Revolutionary Agreements**. While those of us who practice the Agreements experience greater peace in our lives, we have only to look at the news to see that many people are stressed to the max at home, at work, and in a world that sometimes seems unbearable. The good news is that as more of us practice using conscious agreements, we can shift the collective consciousness towards greater Peace on Earth.

Quantum physics has laid the groundwork for us to know our interconnectedness in a way that reflects the teachings of wisdom traditions. Science has shown that we are not separate from one another; rather each one of us is an aspect of a greater whole. Albert Einstein and many other scientists have demonstrated that matter is actually an entanglement of energy waves, and that human consciousness is a part of it.[2]

Neuroscience suggests that each of us can build new habits of thought that result in perceiving reality differently. My own experience consistently verifies this.[3]

The power of practicing these conscious agreements is undeniable. By embodying these Agreements, we can create greater peace in our own lives and thus personally experience greater Peace on Earth *now*. When enough of us do so together, we will be a collective force to shift the prevailing societal paradigm of negativity to that of positivity and possibility.

David R. Hawkins, MD, PhD, showed scientifically in his doctoral thesis and associated book *Power vs. Force* that the power of a few individuals practicing positive states of consciousness like acceptance and joy can counterbalance huge numbers of people living with lower states of consciousness like shame and fear.[4]

We can be those few individuals. You and me and the thousands of others using the Agreements can counterbalance millions. At the core of my being, I know this to be true. That is why I am writing this second edition.

The subtitle of the first edition of *Revolutionary Agreements* is "Twelve Ways to Transform Stress and Struggle into Freedom and Joy." This second edition moves us up a rung on the evolutionary spiral to show us "A Personal Path to Peace on Earth." I am delighted we are on this path together.

# $\mathcal{B}$IRTH OF THE REVOLUTIONARY AGREEMENTS

*I don't personally trust any revolution where love*
*is not allowed.*
—Maya Angelou

While a freshman in college, I created my own definition of Peace: *a state in which each of us naturally desires everyone's well-being and celebrates the beauty in diversity.* Sixteen years later, while participating in a personal development program called Money & You, I had my first glimmer of this state.[1]

One year later, I moved to Boulder to live with my husband, Glenn. Inspired by principles we had learned in Money & You, we initiated a forum called Geneva Group with friends and colleagues who wanted to support each other in living by these principles.[2] We developed our first version of the Agreements in June 1985. Once a month for twenty years, Geneva Group gathered for a full day. We began each gathering by reading the Agreements aloud and exploring their impact on us and our colleagues, friends, and families. As we evolved over the years, so did the Agreements.

In the late 1980s, as the Cold War drew to a close, these Agreements became a foundation for my work as Program Coordinator for a groundbreaking conference among Soviet and American citizen-leaders.[3] Shortly thereafter, the magic of these

Agreements landed Glenn and me among the world's foremost parliamentarians and spiritual leaders—including H.H. the Dalai Lama, Mother Teresa, and then President Mikhail Gorbachev—to co-facilitate their engagement with each other for the benefit of the world.[4]

Glenn and I also took these Agreements to our business clients, where we pioneered leading-edge processes for team building and organizational development on every scale, ranging from small family businesses to the Fortune 50. During the next decade, the Agreements were adapted and adopted by the leaders of more than 250,000 independent sales associates as their Leadership Agreements.

In 1991, I placed a copyright on our Agreements in order to protect our right to use them forever, dubbing them "Revolutionary Agreements."

From that moment on, the Agreements have taken on a life of their own, appearing in various forms in places unreached directly by us. We were delighted to discover, for example, that the Agreements were posted on the office wall of the president of one of the world's largest corporations. Framed posters of the Agreements hang in health care reception and examination areas, living rooms, and work cubicles. One reader reported that she affixed a poster to the ceiling above her bed! She said she wanted the Agreements to be the last thing she saw before closing her eyes for sleep—and the first upon awakening.

The Agreements have been published (in various stages of development) in books and policy documents, including: *Blueprint for Presidential Transition*, a document prepared for President Clinton's transition team;[5] *What is the Emperor Wearing? Truth-Telling in Business Relationships* by Laurie Weiss;[6] *Love Styles: Re-Engineering Marriage for the New Millennium* by Brian Brook;[7] *The Co-Creator's Handbook: An Experiential Guide for*

*Discovering Your Life's Purpose and Building a Co-Creative Society* by Carolyn Anderson and Katharine Roske,[8] and *Living Grace: Spiritual Growth in the Everyday World* by Martie McMane.[9]

These Agreements have helped guide the collaborative efforts of thousands of participants in local gatherings and international conferences, including the Soviet-American Citizens' Summits in Washington, DC and Moscow; the Voices of the Earth eco-spirituality conference in Boulder; and the Summit on Spirituality and Sustainability in Vancouver, BC.

Most of all, the Agreements have made and continue to make extraordinary impacts on the lives of those who post them on their walls, hold them in their hearts, and live by them.

# The One Agreement

If you were to embrace just one Revolutionary Agreement and practice it with diligence, that alone could transform your world. The truth is, practicing any one of these Agreements will tend to lead, in time, to the others because they are interconnected. At their core, they all are facets of the same One Agreement.

What is that One? It has been called many things by many people. Its premise forms the central message at the heart of major world religions.[1] While no single phrase can adequately capture its essence, I might say that the One Agreement is this:

*I agree to be my Self.*

Why the capital "S" in "my Self"? To give it the Divine quality it deserves. To remind us that we each emanate from a Divine source, that our lives are a gift from our Creator and how we choose to live is a gift to our Creator—and indeed to all Creation.

As I simplified and clarified the Agreements for broader use, I began to have glimpses of this underlying unity. The Agreements, which originally numbered sixteen, were distilled to twelve. Those twelve then settled into three groups, representing three core principles—Truth, Acceptance, and Gratitude—which in turn are three facets of the One Agreement.

*I agree to be my Self.*
*I agree to . . .*
*be who I am (Truth);*
*accept others for who they are (Acceptance); and*
*appreciate the gift of this moment (Gratitude).*

When I first read *The Four Agreements* by don Miguel Ruiz in 2001, I was immediately struck by the similarities in the wisdom of Ruiz's book and the essence of our Agreements. I marveled that although Ruiz's and my paths are naturally quite different, the truths to which our Agreements pointed are deeply aligned.[2]

Unlike Ruiz, I claim no ancient wisdom tradition nor a particular spiritual authority. My path to these principles has been through the pragmatic worlds of business, education, government service, and citizen-diplomacy, as well as by grappling with the less lofty daily realities of marriage, parenthood, and friendships.

Nevertheless, encountering Ruiz's work only further affirmed the direction our own work was heading. Ultimately, Ruiz's *Four Agreements* and these twelve Revolutionary Agreements can be said to point to One Agreement: *I agree to be my Self.*

I describe the principles behind the Revolutionary Agreements through true stories—not extraordinary events, just the stuff of everyday life. I also have sought to add perspective, depth, and flavor by offering a selection of quotations from others wiser and more eloquent than I following each Agreement. Finally, at the conclusion of each chapter, I offer you a way to anchor the corresponding Agreement in your own life today.

As you read, I imagine that stories and situations from your own life may emerge that help make the Agreements come alive for you. You may want to jot notes in the margin to capture these situations as they occur to you. You'll also find it useful to keep a journal handy for the "Focus on Today" practices, which appear at the end of each chapter.

Some Agreements may seem quite obvious. Others may feel like too much to deal with right now. You can skip over those if desired and return to them later. As with Goldilocks and the

Three Bears' beds, some Agreements will feel "just right," giving you valuable insights you can implement in your life right away. Some readers have shared that they keep the book on their nightstand or on their breakfast table, where they open it to a random page each day to discover what may be supportive to focus on that day.

The Agreements are not my personal invention or creation. I am but one of their stewards. They are not static; they evolve and continually take on new meanings, becoming richer with experience as we grow and develop. They begin as guidelines— and end as wisdom.

Some you already may know intimately; others will deepen in significance as you explore how they apply in your life. All are timeless. And timely.

# Living a Positive Life

These Agreements may seem simple. Yet following them is not necessarily simple—and certainly not always easy. In a world in which we are bombarded with negative images, words, and actions, it takes courage to live a positive life.

Is it worth it?

My friends and business associates often tell me they think I live a "blessed life." While I acknowledge that blessings, luck, or "good karma" may play a role, I attribute much of my good fortune to living by these simple, powerful Agreements.

Like everyone, I juggle work, family, friendships, household, hobbies, finances, and personal and spiritual growth. In each of these areas, I regularly am challenged by a complex web of circumstances and relationships. Yet as I have followed these Agreements (with more success sometimes than at other times), and as I have reexamined and reabsorbed them, they have served as a powerful guide on my journey to create greater peace in my life and ultimately to cocreate Peace on Earth.

Living by these Agreements as best I can has allowed me to create a life filled with moments of such love that I can hardly contain my laughter or tears . . . and often don't. I enjoy a life of meaningful friendships, richly fulfilling work, and constantly increasing insights about who I am and how you and I and all of humanity are connected. The Revolutionary Agreements have allowed me to create a life that works.

So, yes—it's worth it!

I hope you will live by these Agreements for your own sake. May you experience more loving relationships with your family and friends, a more creative and productive professional life, and greater ease in resolving issues that may be keeping you from fulfilling your unique creative expression and contribution.

My greatest hope is that you will not only live and benefit from these Agreements personally, but that you will also be their spokesperson and advocate, becoming a Revolutionary Leader in cocreating Peace on Earth.

The possibilities for your life are great beyond measure, both for your own fulfillment and for your positive influence on the world around you. Whether you are a public figure who touches millions with your actions and words, or a private person who touches just one other person (who then touches another, who touches another), I know you have the potential—through the expression of living your own life of truth, acceptance, and gratitude—to change the world.

Enjoy the journey!

# *R*EVOLUTIONARY *A*GREEMENTS

## *T*RUTH

### *I AGREE TO*

Live my mission.
Speak my truth, with compassion.
Look within when I react.
Keep doing what works and change what doesn't.

## *A*CCEPTANCE

### *I AGREE TO*

Listen with my heart.
Respect our differences.
Resolve conflicts directly.
Honor our choices.

## *G*RATITUDE

### *I AGREE TO*

Give and receive thanks.
See the best in myself and others.
Look for blessings in disguise.
Lighten up!

# TRUTH

*During times of universal deceit,*
*telling the truth becomes a revolutionary act.*
—George Orwell

# TRUTH

*I AGREE TO:*

*Live my mission.*
*Speak my truth, with compassion.*
*Look within when I react.*
*Keep doing what works and change*
*what doesn't.*

The trinity that underlies these twelve Agreements is rooted in the idea of truth. And by "truth," I mean *your truth*.

*Your truth* is what is true for you, right now. It may not necessarily be true for me, or at least not entirely so, but that doesn't mean it isn't true for you. What's more, your truth today may be somewhat different from your truth a year ago, a month ago, or even yesterday. Our curious nature can lead us to expand our thinking beyond previous self-imposed limitations. As we do, we discover a magnificent world of infinite possibilities. This makes life interesting!

Nonetheless, it can be hard to accept change. This is one reason we often hold onto relationships, jobs, and other situations even when they no longer "ring true" for us. Yet our integrity—being centered in the truth of who we are in this moment—is at the core of a well-lived life.

A magnificent synonym for "your truth" is *authenticity*. Thus, the "One Agreement" could read: *I agree to be my authentic Self.* The principles of truth and authenticity rightfully lie at the heart of all twelve Revolutionary Agreements.

# $\mathcal{A}$GREEMENT ONE

# I agree to live my mission.

*To believe in something, and not to live it, is dishonest.*
—Mahatma Gandhi

Have you ever heard yourself say, "Someday, when I have the time (energy, money, emotional strength), I'll ..."? How would you finish that sentence? For some people, it might be, "take up painting." Or it might be, "go on a cross-country trip ... read great books just for pleasure ... take my kids camping ... study to be an architect ... go on a spiritual retreat ... move to a location I truly love." Whatever it is, it's something you really want to do.

But when? When you retire? When you have the money? When the kids grow up? When you have some "free time"? For most people, the sad truth is that "someday" never comes.

Now, here's the really good news: if "someday" seems impossibly far off, we always have *today*. Everyone does. In fact, today is the *only* day and this moment is the *only* moment we have for certain. What if you could feel fulfilled today, rather than waiting for tomorrow? In a very real sense, you can. How? By identifying what it is that you love, what is truly important to you, then letting that guide your daily actions.

This Agreement completely frees us from the "someday" trap. It asks us to identify our mission, and then live it—right now, today. This Agreement asks us to live our truth—to make our everyday choices and activities an expression of our authentic selves.

Does this mean we can have anything we want right now? No, of course not. But it does mean we can incorporate the *essence* of what we want into our lives in some way, every day, and begin to live the life of our dreams.

When Alice asked the Cheshire Cat which way she should go, he said, "That depends a good deal on where you want to get to." "I don't care much where—" she began to say, and he replied, "Then it doesn't matter which way you go."

What road are you taking? Where does it lead? Asking and answering this question is the first step in creating a life of great fulfillment, its rewards the fruit not of lofty and faraway goals, but of the actions of everyday life.

## What is My Mission?

*Mission* is a magnificent concept. It can relate to visions on the grandest scale, and it can refer to actions that are very practical and immediate. Some people see mission as a calling, a life purpose. For others, being on a mission has to do with accomplishing a specific goal or goals, which may take days, months, or years to achieve.

Your mission may be any of these, all of these, or something else entirely. There is no right way to define mission. Our mission is whatever we choose it to be. And our missions can, and often do, change over time.

Much has been written about the importance of identifying our mission. In *The Co-Creator's Handbook: An Experiential Guide for Discovering Your Life's Purpose*, Carolyn Anderson and

Katharine Roske talk about "being attracted to your chosen work."[1] In *What Should I Do With My Life?*, Po Bronson describes his discovery that our true life mission often comes to us not in a blindingly clear epiphany but, as Bronson puts it, "in a whisper."[2] Learning to follow that whisper may be the most important thing we ever do. In *The 7 Habits of Highly Effective People*[3] and again in *First Things First*,[4] Stephen Covey beautifully explains how easily our mission—those things that are most important to us—can be crowded out of our lives if we let the trivia and minutiae of everyday life take precedence.

However you choose to explore, examine, and define your mission, the critical thing is to do it, then ask yourself this all-important question, "Am I living the essence of this mission every day?"

Your mission needn't be something carved in stone. My own mission has changed many times, and it continues to evolve as I do. Sometimes it is accomplishment-oriented: *To give millions of people tools for cocreating Peace on Earth.* Sometimes it is focused on how I live in the present: *To enjoy life and experience love in every moment.*

Here are some examples of mission statements that have guided me over the years. Some are rather lofty; some are simple, practical, yet profoundly life-changing:

- To facilitate the alignment of leaders.
- To foster an environment of genuine collaboration in which everyone feels empowered to express their individual and collective potential.
- To raise a child who is able to make wise decisions about his health and safety and who is capable of giving and receiving love.
- To be a supportive, loving partner.
- To liberate myself and all humanity to realize our full potential.

- To make a positive difference in the life of each person I meet.
- To foster a growing network of people who choose to be physically, emotionally, spiritually, and financially healthy.

Feel free to use one of these mission statements if it feels right for you, adapt one of them to fit you better, or create one that speaks from your own heart. And don't get hung up on the word "mission." Simply consider what gives you great joy and fulfillment. Take some time to wander through your fondest dreams, visions, and goals. Perhaps ask yourself, "What would I do/be/have if I had all the time and money in the world?" Write down the words that come to you.

Ask yourself, "What do I really want?" and when you have an answer, ask yourself again, "What do I *really* want?" Continue to "peel the layers of the onion" until you feel you have reached the core, the *essence* of your mission.

## What Do I *Really* Want?

_____

_____

_____

_____

_____

So, I might say my mission in life is:

_____

_____

_____

_____

*"I Agree to Live My Mission" is significant for me. I am here as an "encourager," one who supports people to reconnect with their creative spirit so that it permeates all parts of their lives making work, play, and home more rewarding. My mission is important to me, and living it daily fulfills me.*
*—Susie*

## Living Courageously

Simply *identifying* your mission can have revolutionary results all by itself. Your mission may make itself felt and start working its magic in your life right away.

You may discover that once you've taken the time to sit down and write out a statement of your mission, vision, or purpose, that what you've written doesn't jibe with your everyday life. You may want to make some changes … possibly even big changes.

This may require courage. Indeed, as I mentioned in the introduction, it can take courage to live a positive life—and I encourage you to do it. Both *courage* and *encourage* come from the root word, *cor*, which means "heart." Having the courage to find and live your mission means following your heart—putting your heart into it.

*Reading* Revolutionary Agreements *turned a light on in my heart and made me realize that I had not been in alignment with my true desire, which is to be an agent of peace. Leaving behind over 30 years of the familiar corporate world and stepping out into a vast unknown, I discovered a feeling I call "joyful terror." I wanted to sustain myself*

> *spiritually as well as financially—only this time by doing something I love.*
>
> *My strong spirituality plus the newly acquired tools I learned from* Revolutionary Agreements *bolstered my courage to recreate my destiny at 57 . . . I am enjoying this new roller coaster ride and rejoice in the feeling of fulfillment that comes from doing what I love. By working with the Agreements in Truth, Acceptance, and Gratitude I am becoming that agent of peace.*
>
> *—Ed*

Sometimes people discover that the mission of the organization they work for is not consistent with their personal values; in other words, they may be in the wrong place. If you are unhappy in your workplace, could it be that you are uncomfortable trying to live your company's mission?

As organizational development consultants, my husband, Glenn, and I often warned company executives that when we completed our team vision and values work, some of their employees (or even the executives themselves) might choose to leave the organization.

We once offered this cautionary note to the CEO of a company with about forty employees. She replied that she understood and that it was all right. She would rather have only those people who were dedicated to her mission. After we had completed our work with her company, several employees did indeed choose to leave. One of these was a woman who said, "I'm going to sell my house, get an RV, and write my book." She had discovered that she didn't connect to the mission of the organization with which she was working. She felt she was wasting her life by not living her own mission.

This woman was no longer willing to settle for "someday." By identifying what she wanted to be doing *today*, she also left the company in a stronger position, with greater solidarity of purpose among the remaining employees. This woman's brave decision to follow her heart and live her mission resulted in a win for her *and* a win for the company.

## Putting My Mission to the Test

At the age of 34, I identified my first personal mission: *To facilitate the alignment of leaders.* This clarified desire soon played a defining role in an important life decision. Indeed, it turned out to have a major impact on the rest of my life.

Glenn and I had just finished a two-year business consulting contract away from home, and I was ready to make my next major work commitment. Just then, two situations came my way. I was offered a well-paying contract with a major company to help develop a consumer guide. At the same time, a good friend, Barbara Marx Hubbard, asked if we would help her complete preparations for a forthcoming Soviet-American Citizens' Summit to be held in Washington, DC.

The first offer promised all the benefits of a great professional contract. It would engage me in work that utilized my technical writing skills, was close to home, and paid well. If I accepted the second offer instead, I would have to leave home for three months of long days on a project that was behind schedule—and for which I would need to raise funds in order to bring my team with me. At the same time, there was also a certain nobility of purpose and historic dimension to this second option, which was attractive to me.

As I wrestled with this decision, Glenn asked me, "Which situation more closely matches your personal mission? Which is more likely to help you *facilitate the alignment of leaders?*" In other words, Glenn held up the yardstick of Agreement One.

It was no contest.

Little did I know where this short-term commitment would lead. During those three months, President Reagan and President Gorbachev met to move the Cold War toward its end. Our bringing together citizens from former enemy states to create and collaborate on joint projects helped dismantle stereotypes and subtly reshaped history. During an auspicious week in 1988 in Washington, DC, Soviet and American citizen-leaders built relationships as they explored and discovered ways to work together in their chosen fields of interest, be it agriculture, medicine, religion and spirituality, education, the arts, or another area represented by one of the twenty-one task forces. They initiated relationships that deepened over the course of the more than three hundred projects that emerged that week and continued for many years, including annual multinational conferences on education; shared computer technology for environmentally-sound practices; a joint study on the treatment of war trauma; projects promoting new Soviet entrepreneurial activities; collaborative films to expose and eliminate stereotypes; peaceful exchanges among military personnel from different nations; telecommunications projects; and space education.

And it didn't stop there. I could not have predicted it at the time, but my decision also opened the door to many more years of fulfilling my mission in other situations—situations I likely never would have discovered otherwise.

Because of our work on the Soviet-American Citizens' Summit, our team was invited to help design the first Global Forum of Spiritual and Parliamentary Leaders on Human Survival in Oxford, England, and then the second Global Forum on the Environment in Moscow. These Summits brought together some of the greatest minds and hearts of our generation—people typically kept apart—to collaborate on the future of our world.

During these events, we had the privilege of serving such leaders as Mother Teresa, H.H. the Dalai Lama, the Archbishop of Canterbury, Hopi Elder Thomas Banyacya, Iroquois Chief Oren Lyons, the Very Reverend James Parks Morton, renowned scientist Carl Sagan, US Senator Al Gore, esteemed cabinet members from countries all over the world, and Soviet President Mikhail Gorbachev, who hosted the closing event of the 1990 Global Forum at the Kremlin.

Would any of these opportunities have come into my life if I hadn't clearly defined and followed my personal mission? I highly doubt it. I am an ordinary person who simply took the time to consider what makes me feel really good, wrote this down as a personal mission statement, and then used it to guide my actions.

## Your Mission Lives in the Present

The focus of Agreement One is not on accomplishing a specific mission or goal, but rather on the impact our missions have on our everyday lives. In other words, the importance of your mission is not to *achieve* it, but to *live* it; not to *wish for* it, but to *personify* it.

There is a huge distinction between the two—and recognizing that distinction can make all the difference in the world. This happened, in fact, when I initially arrived at the site of preparations for the first Soviet-American Citizens' Summit.

The Summit's stated mission was: *To deepen relationships between Soviet and American citizens by creating and collaborating on joint projects serving their nations and the world.* When I first walked into that office (just blocks from the Hart Senate Office Building where I'd worked a few years earlier) with only three months remaining before the event, I was stunned by the contrast between mission and current reality.

41

Despite the lofty mission, the Summit's office environment looked like so many others I had encountered. Chaos reigned. Tensions were high. Communication was strained. All eyes were on the clock as it ticked away, the three-month deadline looming ominously. There was more work to be done than these intelligent, dedicated, and caring people could possibly complete in time. Everyone was getting burned out.

When Glenn and I arrived, we invited the staff to take a breath. We took them off-site for a day of remembering—remembering what they had hoped this mission would accomplish and how they had felt when they first began working together for this noble cause. They reconnected with the essence of the Summit's mission: *To deepen relationships . . . by creating and collaborating on joint projects . . .*

If the staff had been living that mission every day, they naturally would have experienced deepening relationships amongst themselves as they collaborated on creating the forthcoming Summit. Of course, this would have served the organization's mission as well. However, without a process to illuminate this connection, the organization's powerful mission was lost in the hustle and bustle of daily preparations and relegated to a hope for the future, rather than serving as a guide for today.

Glenn and I introduced the Agreements to the staff, and we worked collectively to adapt them to serve the special needs of this extraordinary project. Everyone agreed to take time each morning to gather together and listen as each member of the team read one Agreement aloud. We began by reading the mission of the Summit and recommitting ourselves to *live* that mission.

Due to the brilliant inspiration and historic efforts of Rama Jyoti Vernon, Director of the Center for Soviet-American Dialogue, and Barbara Marx Hubbard, the Summit's visionary Program Chairperson, the results were magnificent. Hundreds of projects were born or fostered that February, many of which continued to expand in the ensuing years. The Summit staff walked their talk by living their mission; as a result, they changed the world.

## Mission in the Workplace

Think for a moment about your place of work. Do you know your organization's mission?

Let's suppose you work for a company with a mission that includes the words "to surprise and delight our customers." How might you live this mission every day?

What would you expect to observe in a workplace where everyone lived the mission: *To surprise and delight our customers*? Would you be more likely to hear, "Sorry, that's not my job" or, "Sure, I'll be glad to help!"? Would you expect to see people meeting the minimum required of them or striving to do their very best? Would you see people plodding dully through their tasks, or would you witness the sparkle of creativity flowing? Might you see spontaneous celebrations when the customers were surprised and delighted? (And wouldn't that delight you?)

In the business classic, *The E-Myth Revisited: Why Most Small Businesses Don't Work and What to Do About It*, author Michael Gerber describes his experience of staff members embodying their mission at a resort hotel he happened upon one night.[5]

The hotel's objective was to give their customers a sense that this was a special place, created by special people, doing what they do in the best possible way. How did that manifest? During the brief check-in process, the clerk made a reservation for Michael in the hotel restaurant. After his meal, he enjoyed a brandy. Returning to his room eager to light a fire in the fireplace on this chilly night, he found the fire already ablaze, his bed turned down, and in addition to the usual mints, there was another glass of brandy by his bedside.

Michael also discovered a card welcoming him for his first stay and inviting to him to call day or night with any needs. In the morning, in response to a polite knock on his door, he discovered a newspaper. But not just any newspaper—his favorite newspaper.

These actions and others like them not only surprised and delighted Michael—they also turned him into a customer for life. The employees at that hotel not only knew the hotel's mission; they lived it.

The following is from Reverend Martie McMane's book, *Living Grace: Spiritual Growth in the Everyday World.* This is the first of several wonderful stories I'll share from her book about the impact of the Agreements in her life.[6]

*[I introduced to] the church council ... the concept of people only being called forth to do those things that they had energy for, things that excited them, things that gave them joy and satisfaction. It sounded like a great idea to keep people from burnout, to keep people from getting grumpy, resentful, and angry.*

*Then at one of our meetings, the head of the trustees said, "This sounds all well and good, but let's get practical. Who's gonna do the windows?" We had a contemporary sanctuary with two whole walls of floor-to-ceiling windows on each side. Of course, everyone laughed.*

*And I said, "Well, if no one comes forth who likes to do windows, we'll just have to pull the curtains for a while so we don't notice them."*

*And wouldn't you know it? At our next new members class, when we were talking about where people might like to offer their energy for the ministries of the church, one of the women said, "I do windows." I'm not kidding. She loved to do windows, she said, because she could see what she had done. It gave her a sense of accomplishment.*

*—Martie*

What if you and your work team were to spend a few hours together in a relaxed setting to explore the question, "How could we live our mission today?" How might this enhance your work life? And how might this strategy positively affect the people who are the beneficiaries of your organization's mission?

## Mission in the Schools

My son's elementary school, Eagle Crest, had a mission fashioned around an acrostic for "Eagle":

Expect nothing less than success.

Always think before we act.

Grow and learn in new and different ways.

Learn to accept responsibility for our actions.

Everyone practices kindness and consideration.

Imagine if every school's staff members—principals, teachers, administrative staff, cafeteria staff, and janitors—lived such a mission as a model for our children and our communities. If school administrators were to truly "expect nothing less than success," they would hold their teachers and our children in the highest esteem, expecting all of them to reach the height of their potential.

What if practicing "kindness and consideration" were regularly noticed and rewarded? How might this affect the choices our children make? Indeed, Michael's school did practice this. As a result, the children often were rewarded when the principal caught them doing something that exceeded their daily pledge of this mission statement. My son was delighted to be invited to lunch in the cafeteria with the principal more than once!

# Mission in the Family

What kind of impact would it have if you and your family created a *family mission statement*? What would you like to accomplish together? What kind of interactions would you like to have?

Regardless of our backgrounds, we share one thing in common: at the core of our being is a desire to love and be loved. What if each of us consciously chose to include "loving" as part of our personal mission? And what if we let this mission guide our daily actions? Surely our lives would never be the same. Indeed, we would have changed our world in the blink of an eye.

On the next page is a mission statement that Glenn, our then nine-year-old son, Michael, and I wrote for our family. We then laminated it and displayed it prominently in our home.

"I agree to live my mission" is the first of these twelve pathways for living a positive life. Take the time to consider how to embody this agreement so that rather than working toward fulfilling your mission, your mission gives you the fulfillment you deserve *today*.

# TO LOVE AND RESPECT
## - A 15 YEAR PACT -

We, Michael Justin Head, Marian Linda Head and Glenn Eugene Head, enter into this agreement on July 4, 1999 with gladness and joy. We choose to treat each other with respect, honoring each other as the unique individuals we are. Although there are times when we may disagree, we will refrain from being nasty and mean, endeavoring to always be loving and respectful.

We understand that there may be times that we forget this agreement, and we ask of each other that we be gently reminded, and allowed 24 hours to fully remember and begin once again to treat each other with respect. We will always forgive each other these short lapses, and remember that we are family, forever bonded in love through God our Creator.

By signing below, we show our agreement to treat each other with love and respect for 15 years, at which time this agreement is renewable.

Michael Justin Head    Marian Linda Head    Glenn Eugene Head

# Words of Wisdom

*"I agree to live my mission."*

*Cherish your visions. Cherish your ideals.*
*Cherish the music that stirs in your heart, the beauty that*
*forms in your mind, the loveliness that drapes your purest*
*thoughts, for out of them will grow all delightful conditions,*
*all heavenly environment; of these, if you but remain true*
*to them, your world will at last be built.*
—James Allen

*Man's ideal state is realized when he has fulfilled the purpose*
*for which he is born. And what is it that reason demands*
*of him? Something very easy—that he live in accordance*
*with his own nature.*
—Seneca

*When you are making a success of something,*
*it's not work. It's a way of life.*
—Andrew Granatelli

*I dream my painting, and then I paint my dream.*
—Vincent van Gogh

*First say to yourself what you would be;*
*and then do what you have to do.*
—Epictetus

*All know the way; few actually walk it.*
—Bodhidharma

*How wonderful it is that nobody need wait a single moment*
*before starting to improve the world.*
—Anne Frank

*The single most important thing*
*you can do in business is to be yourself.*
—Sherry Lansing

*Concentrate all your thoughts on the task at hand.*
*The sun's rays do not burn until brought to a focus.*
—Alexander Graham Bell

*Here is a test to find whether your mission on earth is finished:*
*If you're alive, it isn't.*
—Richard Bach

*When you discover your mission, you will feel its demand.*
*It will fill you with enthusiasm*
*and a burning desire to get to work on it.*
—W. Clement Stone

*There are three tasks that matter in this lifetime.*
*The first task, though not the most important task,*
*is to quiet the busyness in your mind.*
*The second is to find your song.*
*And the third task is to sing your song.* [7]
—Harry Roberts

*Don't ask yourself what the world needs. Ask yourself*
*what makes you come alive and then go do that. Because what*
*the world needs is people who have come alive.*
—Reverend Dr. Howard Thurman

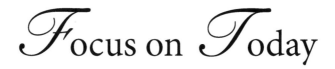

# Focus on Today

*I agree to live my mission—TODAY!*

*Here are a few simple steps you can take to more fully live the truth of who you are, today and every day. Write your answers in your journal—then follow your heart's desire.*

1. My mission (passion, purpose, vision, or dream) is to:
   *Example: Cocreate Peace on Earth.*

2. What is the essence of my mission?
   *Example: To experience Peace on Earth.*

3. What are three ways I can experience the essence of my mission every day?
   *Example:*
   1. *Spend time in Nature daily.*
   2. *Stay present with whatever or whoever is in front of me.*
   3. *Demonstrate living my life in truth, acceptance, and gratitude.*

4. What is one small change I can make *today* to live the essence of my mission?

# $\mathcal{A}$GREEMENT TWO

# I agree to speak my truth, with compassion.

*A truth that disheartens because it is true
is of more value than the most stimulating of falsehoods.*
—Maurice Maeterlinck

While the first Agreement focuses on our actions, the second focuses on our words. The two go hand in hand; authenticity in both deed and word is the manifestation of being true to your Self.

The phrase "my truth" is important here: It is what is true *for me*—my personal opinions, perspectives, and beliefs. When we understand that truth is relative, we can speak our own truth without malice, judgment, or the piercing arrows of "I'm right. You're wrong." Likewise, others are free to speak from their own perspectives, beliefs, and personal opinions: their truth.

## With Compassion

While visiting the Hall of Compassion in Kauai, the tour guide said, "Compassion is the opposite of judgment." I had never heard that definition before, yet it immediately made sense to me. Agreement Two encourages us to hold our tongues if we are about to use words to express judgment of another. When we notice that is our intention, we can instead call upon the Agreement *to look within when I react* to begin the process of releasing our judgment.

When my son, Michael, was a young teen, he attended a special summer program called SuperCamp, in which he was given seven keys to success. One of those keys was "Speak with Good Purpose." A key to success at any age!

"With compassion" also means being sensitive to the people around us. We have our truth, and other people have theirs. Even if we hold wildly different perspectives, we can try to understand one another's perspectives. At the very least, we can be open to the likelihood that our different life experiences (including what may have happened just this morning) influence our perspectives and thus the way we communicate and receive others' communications.

Imagine an infinity symbol passing in the air between you and me. True communication makes a complete loop between the two of us. Communication is not over when a person speaks. It continues as the other person receives and interprets it, giving it personal meaning. The listener's interpretation is filtered by past experiences, values, beliefs, and fears. Each of us has a unique set of these! No wonder communication can be so challenging.

When speaking my truth with compassion, I aim to communicate honestly and in a manner that respects the other person as an individualized expression of the Divine. The essence of this Agreement might be summed up in two words: *kindhearted honesty.*

# What We Fear

Why doesn't everyone speak his or her truth?

For me, fear of rejection kept me from consistently speaking my truth in my younger years. With a deep need to feel accepted, I often used words as a shield of armor rather than a portal to my inner light. Yet this type of armor tends to have the opposite effect of its desired intention. It doesn't generate close, fulfilling relationships. Instead, it blocks the light that emanates from us when we love and accept ourselves.

When we speak in ways that are inauthentic or untruthful, it can repel those who are sensitive enough to feel that something "isn't quite right" with our communication. What "isn't quite right" is that our words are not aligned with our truth, our authentic Self.

For many years I showed up as the person I believed others expected me to be. I was a chameleon, changing my persona depending on the situation or the people in front of me. When I took the time to learn more about who I truly am, I discovered my passion for being "Love in Action." Love doesn't need to exaggerate or tell falsehoods. I decided I would be happier having fewer friends who liked me for who I truly am than many friends who liked me for who I pretended to be. The funny thing is that the quantity of my friends increased, along with the quality.

Another reason some of us button up rather than speak our truth is the fear of creating animosity, as well as a desire to maintain harmony at all costs. My father was adamant that, "Nothing's worth fighting about. It's more important to keep the peace." This certainly had an impact on the way I handled conflict—or more accurately, how I didn't for many years.

One of the reasons children lie is to stay out of trouble. My son told me, "I learned to lie in fourth grade when I found out that if I didn't lie, I would get into trouble." Teaching our children values can be complicated, especially because values often compete with each other. Stay safe or tell the truth? In our family, we put the highest value on honesty, so that's what we got from Michael. In his school culture, he chose differently. I have pondered what would have happened if he had told the truth at school, with compassion. Would he indeed have gotten into trouble, or not? Might he have brought an important new perspective to his teacher? Michael's truth-telling certainly has opened my eyes over the years. Indeed, his honesty has been one of my greatest teachers.

Staying safe and secure is a prime reason why some people don't tell the truth at work even when lives depend on it. Some years ago, there was a report of copilots being reticent to tell their pilots the truth for fear of insubordination even when a fatal accident could be the result. In some cases, when crewmembers pointed out problems, the senior pilot ignored them. Could these crewmembers have spoken their truth more boldly and assertively without fear of jeopardizing their jobs?

In January 2015, after four incidents of flight crew errors that were classified as "major safety events and near-misses," United Airlines sent their pilots a memo entitled, "SAFETY ALERT: Significant safety concerns." Here's an excerpt, "Every time we enter the cockpit with the intention of performing our pilot duties, we evaluate risk. Every pilot must be willing to speak up if safety is in question. In the same vein, every pilot must also accept the input of their fellow crewmembers on the flight deck. In most cases, one of the pilots recognizes an unsafe situation. In some cases, a pilot's input is ignored. This is unacceptable."[1]

## Truth at Work

Can you see how readily this Revolutionary Agreement could transform the workplace? Imagine what life could be like if your teammates, employees, supervisors, and peers all told you their truth—with compassion?

I learned from my friend and mentor Barbara Marx Hubbard to think of each of my work teams as an astronaut corps. If I were an astronaut, would I withhold my truth about my teammates' performance? No way! If we depended on each other for our very lives, you'd better believe we'd be telling each other the truth— with or without compassion. And here's a striking thought: we *do* depend on each other for our lives, or at least for the quality of our lives. The choices we make—from how we show up at work to where we shop to how we treat our neighbors—have impacts far beyond our immediate view.

Astronaut corps are comprised of people with diverse backgrounds and experience. The crew of the space shuttle Columbia included men and women who were black, brown, and white; Hindu, Roman Catholic, Jewish, Charismatic Christian, Unitarian, Episcopalian, and Baptist; Indian, Israeli, and American. Each brought unique perspectives (personal truths), yet each was committed to the highest level of personal excellence and teamwork towards the accomplishment of their shared mission.[2]

The diversity of our teams creates fertile ground for creativity, innovation, synergy, and excellence. When teammates learn to speak their truth with compassion (not judgment), the possibilities for personal and collective success are limitless.

## Telling the Truth to Our Customers

Truthful relationships with our customers is vital. One of the early challenges I faced in my network marketing career was overcoming the image of sales as a profession that depended on manipulating the truth. (My mother reveals this common bias, for example, when she used to introduce me to others by explaining what I did—then adding, with an obvious mix of delight, pride, and incredulity, "And she always tells the truth.")

My business associates and customers often tell me that my success is due in large part to my authenticity and the honest, straightforward way I present my products and business opportunities. I continue to be amazed and saddened by businesspeople who feel they must exaggerate the truth in order to achieve success, even when their products and services would stand perfectly well enough on their own merits.

Consider relationships you have as a customer or client of others. Are the enduring ones built upon a strong foundation of trust? Is that trust based upon honest communications? A key ingredient in sustaining business success is the potent, positive force of relationships built upon honesty and integrity.

## Little White Lies

Sadly, many have come to expect that people don't tell the truth and that living with lies is normal, especially "little white lies." Telling little white lies is a seductive thing. We do this ostensibly to avoid hurting other people's feelings or to avoid some other sort of conflict, so the practice can appear to have noble motivation.

Yet it is a profoundly destructive habit. Why so? Because it undermines trust. When people hear you speak little white lies, they don't know when or if they can ever believe you. This applies whether they discover your white lie spoken directly to them or they overhear it spoken to another. For example, when a child hears a parent speak an obvious falsehood to her sibling, it plants seeds of distrust—does the parent lie to her as well? Telling white lies is like building a house on sand. There's no foundation for your relationship.

Years ago, my mother had a pattern of creating stories to support her actions in which I was cast as the bad guy and she as the angel. It was so subtle that I'm not sure she was even aware of it. "I don't want to visit you for longer than four nights," she might say. "I don't want to be in your way. You're too busy to have company for longer than that."

An uneasy feeling would set in. Where did this "four nights" idea come from? Did I actually say I was too busy? I didn't think so. What was she getting at? Sometimes her statement became round one of a game. My next move would be to show her how much I cared for her by trying to convince her to change her mind and stay longer. It was frustrating. I was being blamed for her decision, and yet I knew darn well she wasn't being completely honest with me.

Finally I asked her outright, "Do you mean you don't want to stay longer than four nights because by then you'll be ready to get home to your friends and your routine? Or do you mean that you don't like it when I don't make time for you when you come to visit?"

The truth was, she meant both of those things at different times, and neither one was easy for her to admit. Eventually we got this all out on the table, and she agreed to be honest with me. She started telling me how much she loved being with me and my family (which was true) and how difficult it was for her to miss too many of her activities with her friends (which was also true). And, she began to ask me when would be the best time for her to visit so that it would only minimally interrupt the work I love (which showed compassion for me).

*The power of the truth is always greater than the reason for the lie.*

Even a young child is wise enough to know the difference between the truth and "little white lies." Six-year-old Michael accompanied Glenn, Glenn's mother, and me on a tour of an assisted living center. As we walked through one room, Michael spied an enormous jar filled with cookies and asked, "May I have one?" Glenn said, "Of course." Michael finished his cookie in the next room, then asked if he might go back and get another—to which Michael's Nana replied, "No." When he started to fuss, she said, "They're all gone." Perplexed by this confusing response, Michael didn't know what to do but pout.

Do we endear ourselves to our children (and grandchildren) by avoiding conflicts through obvious falsehoods . . . or do we instead earn their distrust?

How do you feel when someone says something to you that doesn't ring true? "We're sorry we can't join you for the movie. Suzie has a headache." The speaker may think this is an easy way out that hurts no one. But how much greater trust and deeper friendship would result if he were to say instead, "Thanks so much for inviting us. I'm not interested in this particular movie, but we'd love to join you for a movie another time."

A friendship built upon lies—even those supposedly "harmless little white" ones—is a house of cards. Sooner or later it will fall.

## The Power of Telling the Truth

It is deeply comforting to know you can ask a friend anything, and he or she will always tell you the truth in response. One of my best friends, Peggy, is a great model for living this agreement. "Would you like to come for dinner tonight?" I will ask her.

"No," answers Peggy, "I'm really needing family time tonight. Let's do it another time." No headaches, no excuses. Just the truth. How refreshing!

In addition to establishing a foundation of trust in our friendships, speaking our truth is the most direct path to reestablishing harmony when it has been disrupted or conflict has arisen.

"I feel disconnected from you."

Or, "Something doesn't feel right. What just happened?"

No blame, just a desire to reconnect. Truth maintains an inner integrity that links to integrity in others, forming the angles of the sacred geometry of our relationships. Without integrity, there is no true connection. With truth, relationships can become extraordinary.

*My three sisters and I used to gossip quite a bit. It didn't take me long to recognize the lack of integrity here, and no one seemed inclined to address the issue directly with the target of these conversations. Finally, I simply refused to participate. Our youngest sister asked me about it and I told her truthfully, "I just can't see how anything positive can come from gossiping behind someone's back. If we aren't willing to say the same things to her face, then we should not be saying them behind her back."*

*Speaking my truth did not diminish my sisters' love for me, and they respected my position. As a result, the "gossip fests" are mostly a thing of the past, especially when I am around.*

*—Sigrid*

## Politeness at the Expense of Honesty

When I ask a friend for a favor, I expect her to respond by letting me know honestly whether or not she has both the ability and desire to fulfill it. Unfortunately, many people are raised to be polite to others (a good thing) at the expense of honesty (not such a good thing). This created a major rift once with a good friend, "Linda."

Occasionally I would ask her, "Would you mind if our son stayed at your home for an hour after school, and we'll pick him up later?"

One time, Linda replied, "Sure, I'd love that, but I don't know. I've got to get to the store today to pick up some things." To which I jumped in helpfully, "I'll be going by that store this morning. I'd be happy to pick up what you need!"

I thought I was being helpful. To Linda, this felt manipulative. She thought I should have gotten her hint and withdrawn my request. Since she didn't say a word about it to me, I would never have known her perspective . . . if she hadn't complained to a mutual friend that I was "using her." When the friend shared this with me, I was shocked. I had no idea that my request had been an imposition. I thought angrily, "Why didn't she tell me?" I made a date to get together with Linda to see if we could relieve the mounting tension between us.

I was nervous about the meeting. Our friendship was important to me. I was angry at her behind-my-back talk, confused about why she wouldn't just tell me what was on her mind in the first place, and afraid of the repercussions of this conflict. It turned out to be an enlightening encounter for both of us.

"When someone asks me a favor," Linda explained, "I was taught to always say 'yes.'" Thus, she often felt stuck doing things she didn't want to do. Linda and I placed different values on truth-telling and neighborliness.

We agreed that if Linda had simply said, "It doesn't really work for me to do that today," delivering the message cleanly and without guilt, I would have received and appreciated her honesty. No justification needed; just the simple truth.

After that incident, I said to Glenn, "I'd rather have one or two friends who tell me the truth than a hundred friends who choose politeness over honesty."

## Being True to Ourselves

In my first marriage, I spent many years acting as though everything was just fine, when I actually felt an inner pain burning constantly. Everything was not at all "just fine," but I hadn't the courage to say so.

One day, in a therapy session designed to help my husband and me speak our truths to each other, I surprised us all when suddenly I had an aha moment and blurted out, "I feel like a fake! My whole life feels like a fake!" I had spent years lying about my feelings not only to my husband, but to myself as well. (The ulcers and migraines should have been a clue.)

When I later learned to practice this Agreement in its fullness, the reward was a peacefulness in my heart and my soul that I had not previously experienced. Recognizing and speaking my truth brought with it a sense of being in full integrity. It wasn't easy to break my old fear-based habit, but it was tremendously worth it.

*One of my highest values in a job is working as part of a team. I took a job that seemed great, paid well, and used my skills, but I worked totally alone. I rarely saw my boss let alone anyone else. As time went on, I became more and more uncomfortable yet was not able to face the issue within myself.*

*One day my boss came in and suggested that I seemed unhappy and perhaps the position was not a fit for me. I was immediately fearful of losing my job and responded, "No, I am happy here." My boss gently suggested that I take some time to think about it.*

*I went home and reflected on what had happened. My boss was speaking my truth for me! The next day I called her and said, "You're absolutely right, I'm not happy here." We agreed to end the working relationship and she appreciated my honesty, raved about how much she enjoyed working with me, and gave me flowers as a going away gift.*

> *I spent two weeks training my replacement and that was my happiest time there because I was working with someone. Now I have a different job working with a team for a common goal and I love it!*
>
> *I learned that speaking my truth with compassion is not just telling someone else but acknowledging the truth to myself.*
>
> —*Carol*

## Telling the Truth in Politics

Many of us living in the United States were taught in elementary school that when our first President, George Washington, was a young boy and overly enthusiastic about a new hatchet, he cut down his father's prized cherry tree. When his father demanded to know what happened to his tree, young George confessed and said, "I cannot tell a lie. I cut down your cherry tree." Unfortunately for many of us, our impression of honesty in government has gone downhill ever since

For most of my lifetime, Americans have struggled to deal with dishonesty at all levels of government. Yet what or who is the "government"? As President Lincoln memorialized in his Gettysburg Address, in the US "it is a government of the people, by the people, and for the people."

And who are we, if we are not "the people"? Each of us can begin to affect change, first within ourselves, then in our schools, workplaces, and communities at large. And we can begin by speaking our truth, with compassion.

"The fault, dear Brutus," says Cassius in Shakespeare's *Julius Caesar*, "is not in our stars but in ourselves." And so is the solution. We will enjoy greater honesty in government when we embody it ourselves and expect the same from our elected officials.

Be a leader in your workplace, your home, and your community. When you consistently speak your truth, with compassion for others and yourself, you experience greater peace, wellness, and abundance. Your integrity serves as an example for others, enabling lasting friendships, productive work teams, and governance that truly serves the people.

# Words of Wisdom

*"I agree to speak my truth, with compassion."*

*Truth and tears clear the way*
*to a deep and lasting friendship.*
—Marie de Sévigné

*Level with your child by being honest.*
*Nobody spots a phony quicker than a child.*
—Mary MacCracken

*Where is there dignity unless there is honesty?*
—Marcus Tullius Cicero

*When in doubt, tell the truth. It will confound your enemies*
*and astound your friends.*
—Mark Twain

*Our lives improve only when we take chances*
*and the first and most difficult risk we can take*
*is to be honest with ourselves.*
—Walter Anderson

*If it is not seemly, do it not;*
*if it is not true, speak it not.*
—Marcus Aurelius

*Those who think it is permissible to tell white lies*
*soon grow color-blind.*
—Austin O'Malley

*Have the courage to be sincere, clear, and honest. This opens
the door to deeper communication all around. It creates
self-empowerment and the kind of connections with
others we all want in life.*
—Sara Paddison

*I hope I shall possess firmness and virtue enough
to maintain what I consider the most enviable of all titles,
the character of an honest man.*
—George Washington

*I love you, and because I love you, I would sooner have you hate
me for telling you the truth than adore me for telling you lies.*
—Pietro Aretino

*A lie will easily get you out of a scrape, and yet,
strangely and beautifully, rapture possesses you
when you have taken the scrape and left out the lie.*
—Charles Edward Montague

*We believe that a compassionate world is a peaceful world . . .
that all human beings are born with the capacity for
compassion, and that it must be cultivated for
human beings to survive and thrive.*
—Charter for Compassion International

*I believe that unarmed truth and unconditional love
will have the final word in reality.*
—Martin Luther King, Jr.

# Focus on Today

*I agree to speak my truth, with compassion—*
**TODAY.**

*Here are a few simple steps you can take to enhance your awareness of and practice speaking your truth, with compassion. Record your thoughts in your journal.*

1. Choose three family members and/or friends with whom you frequently interact. Ask yourself and honestly answer each of the following questions as they pertain to each person you've chosen:

   Do I *always* speak to this person honestly, without judgment?

   If the answer is "no" for any of the people you have chosen, then ask yourself:

   > Am I willing to look within to discover what compels me to be dishonest or to judge?

   > When or in what situations will I speak my truth, with compassion to this person?

2. Choose three people from work or the community-at-large with whom you interact the most, and ask yourself the same questions from above in relationship to them.

# $\mathscr{A}$GREEMENT THREE

# I agree to look within when I react.

*It is only imperfection that complains of what is imperfect. The more perfect we are the more gentle and quiet we become towards the defects of others.*
—Joseph Addison

"That person is so mean."
"She is so manipulative."
"He is so prejudiced."

It's one thing to observe someone behaving or speaking negatively; it's another altogether to be *consumed* by our negative feelings about that person or behavior. I've learned the hard way that when someone's actions cause us emotional distress, we have an opportunity for healing—specifically, for healing *ourselves*.

## How I Learned This Agreement

My mother-in-law was visiting us in Colorado. During one evening together, she said so many things I perceived as mean, manipulative, and hurtful that I found myself in a complete frenzy.

I had *never* been spoken to that way! How *could* she! I couldn't stay in my house with her *one moment longer*! What was I to *do*? I frantically searched for a reason to leave for a few days. She was *horrible*! I felt as though I *hated* her!

Experiencing these feelings was especially painful for me. From the time I was young, I always strove to live by my father's advice: *Life is too short to hate anyone.* Hate was an out-of-control, angry, loaded, despicable word I had projected onto another person only one other time in my entire life.

I knew I was in trouble and didn't know where to turn. I prayed . . . and my prayer was answered.

Ahden, a dear friend and psychologist who was staying with us at the time said, "Marian, if you are willing to take a deep, hard look at *yourself*, I can help you."

"What do you mean?" I asked, perplexed and still angry. My friend then revealed the message behind this Agreement.

"When you have such a powerful emotional reaction to what someone else says, it usually has to do with a part of yourself that you don't like."

This was difficult for me to accept. What could she possibly be talking about? I was a *nice* person. I wasn't mean and manipulative. Ahden was patient with me.

"Has there ever been a time when you feel you were manipulative?" I searched inside myself and had to admit that, yes, there had been such a time. "And how do you feel about that part of yourself?" she asked. Not good, I admitted. Uncomfortable. Embarrassed. Hmmm.

"How about mean? Have you ever been mean to someone?" she asked. After considering this, I had to admit that I hadn't always been sugar, spice, and everything nice to my own mother. "And how did you feel about that?" Well, it didn't make me feel like an angel.

Strangely enough, as I began to uncover my hidden self-judgment, rather than feeling worse, I actually began to relax. The anger I felt toward my mother-in-law was dissipating.

"So what do I do about it?" I asked.

"You've already taken a huge step," she explained. "Just being aware that these strong feelings you thought were about your mother-in-law's behavior are really about you should diffuse your anguish about her. What you choose to do about those feelings is up to you."

"You can learn to embrace all parts of yourself," she continued, "knowing that you make the best choice or decision in every moment, given your current circumstances and wisdom. You can change those things about yourself that you don't like. Or you can leave those parts alone, knowing that you just don't like it when you behave that way. It's up to you."

It was a miracle. The next day, I saw my mother-in-law in a completely new light. It wasn't about *her* anymore. The fire burning beneath my explosive emotion had been put out by this new insight. I no longer held her accountable for my feelings.

It simply changed my life.

Shortly after this episode, we added this important Agreement to our Geneva Group list of Agreements. To this day, I continue to be amazed at the potency of its wisdom—and that applying it blows apart my strongest negative emotions directed at other people. Practicing this Agreement has transformed my reactions from anger to compassion, from hate to love.

*Since working with the Agreements, I notice I have fewer reactions to differing opinions, and I am able to more quickly stop myself before laying blame on another. The Agreements remind me to look within for the source of my issue. Once I discover that source, my reaction usually*

> *dissipates. Then I can relax and respect the differences of the other or, if need be, express my truth about the matter at hand–with compassion.*
> —Gail

# We Control Our Own Buttons

Practicing this Agreement has taught me that no one can make me feel a certain way.

In 1984, when a relative was visiting me in Washington, DC, she referred to a group of people by a name I felt was derogatory. I was incensed. Her remarks cut into me and bothered me deeply for a long time.

Years later, when she visited us in Colorado, I noticed something fascinating. She continued to speak in the same way, using this same language—only now I was simply *noticing* it. I didn't care for the racial slur any more now than I had then … but I was no longer having a heightened emotional response.

What was the difference? Back in 1984, *I was still grappling with my own prejudices.* They weren't the same as hers, but prejudice is prejudice. Now, many years and experiences later, I had shed much of my own ignorance and cut the cords of intolerance that had bound me so strongly to her words that had pushed my buttons.

I still didn't care for the terms my relative was using. It's just that her using them no longer pushed my buttons. I also have learned that most things I say to others with a strong emotional charge turn out, upon examination, to be about myself. What I like in others, I tend to like in myself. What I don't like in others tends to relate to what I do not like in myself … even when that's hard to admit.

When someone says, "He really knows how to push my buttons," just what are those buttons anyway, and exactly what are they connected to? I've noticed that my buttons are connected to the feelings I have about myself, typically unresolved feelings that carry a great weight.

When I feel triggered, I have learned to reflect upon the incident as soon as possible. I ask myself, "What about this other person's behavior reminds me of myself?" Once I identify it, I can move forward by simply accepting this part of me or by forgiving myself for that behavior. Regardless of what I choose to do, by taking responsibility for my disproportionate reaction to someone's behavior, I immediately disconnect from feeling judgment about the other person. It's not about them.

This is not an easy Agreement for me to keep. It is much easier to blame someone else for how I feel than to take the time and energy to look within and accept full responsibility for my feelings. Yet how we *feel* is surely one of those precious few areas of our lives over which we *can* claim complete control. Our feelings are our own. Someone can strike out at us and even damage us physically, but no one can grab hold of our feelings and squeeze the life out of them. Only we have the power to allow or disallow this.

*About twenty years ago, I worked with a woman we'll call Frieda who had an amazing amount of positive energy. She was a human dynamo. Busy all the time, she chatted her way through life. She could whistle a happy tune in four parts and smile while doing it. Her energy never stopped. Although twenty-five years older than me, she got up at 5:30 a.m. six days a week so she could make a 6:00 a.m. aerobics class at the Y!*

71

*During this time, I was struggling with fibromyalgia and migraine headache syndrome, along with the fear that I might not be able to continue to work effectively. Frieda's constant energy and "be happy" attitude really started to annoy me. When she bopped down the hall and cheerily stuck her head in my office, I found myself getting very tense. I would smile plastically, then get up and shut the door to avoid hearing her gleeful voice down the hall.*

*When I began to reflect on the negative and critical feelings I was having about Frieda, I ran smack-dab into myself and my own fears. As I examined what was going on inside me, I realized that I was feeling critical of Frieda because I was afraid that I would be judged inadequate. I did not have her energy, so perhaps others would find me lacking. I did not feel positive and cheery, so I was afraid I was not good enough. I was afraid people might think of me as a downer, as I was judging myself to be. And, in fact, I was envious of Frieda's energetic, positive attitude— something I lacked. What I had to do was go inward, admit my own fears, and accept my limitations and imperfections . . . Once I could admit my scary, childlike feelings, things began to change. When I finally realized that my reaction to her was not about her, but was really about me, I was no longer critical of her.*[1]

—*Martie*

## It's Not Personal

When I hear someone make a comment or pass a judgment about me, I now consider that it may be in some way related to that person's concept of themselves. For the most part, I believe we judge others based on what is in our minds and hearts *about ourselves*, and not about the person we are speaking to or about.

Knowing this has dramatically reduced the drama in my life. I used to take people's critical comments to heart, particularly when someone close to me spoke them with great emotion. That was because I thought it was actually about me. No more.

When I first read don Miguel Ruiz's book *The Four Agreements,* I was intrigued and gratified to notice that his Second Agreement is, "Don't take anything personally." He is absolutely right—because it's *not* personal. As he explains, "Nothing other people do is because of you. It is because of themselves. ... Even when a situation seems so personal, even if others insult you directly, it has nothing to do with you. What they say, what they do, and the opinions they give are according to the agreements they have in their own minds."[2]

It's well worth the pain and effort to search for the unresolved issues within us that trigger strong reactions to what others say or do. The results are wisdom, compassion, and love for ourselves and others. All significant steps on our personal path to Peace on Earth.

# Words of Wisdom

*"I agree to look within when I react."*

*When you see a man of worth,*
*think how to rise to his level.*
*When you see an unworthy man,*
*then look within and examine yourself.*
—Confucius

*Know thyself.*
—Ancient Delphic maxim inscribed
at the Temple of Apollo at Delphi

*Many of the faults you see in others, dear reader,*
*are your own nature reflected in them.*
—Rumi

*No man can produce great things*
*who is not thoroughly sincere in dealing with himself.*
—James Russell Lowell

*Turbulence is life force. It is opportunity.*
*Let's love turbulence and use it for change.*
—Ramsey Clark

*Let the refining and improving of your own life*
*keep you so busy that you have*
*little time to criticize others.*
—H. Jackson Brown, Jr.

*The unexamined life is not worth living.*
—Socrates

*Everything that irritates us about others*
*can lead us to an understanding of ourselves.*
—Carl Jung

*A lively, disinterested, persistent looking for truth*
*is extraordinarily rare. Action and faith enslave thought,*
*both of them in order not to be troubled or inconvenienced*
*by reflection, criticism, or doubt.*
—Henri-Frédéric Amiel

*Everyone thinks of changing the world,*
*but no one thinks of changing himself.*
—Leo Tolstoy

*Only by much searching and mining*
*are gold and diamonds obtained,*
*and man can find every truth connected with his being*
*if he will dig deep into the mine of his soul.*
—James Allen

*If you do not tell the truth about yourself*
*you cannot tell it about other people.*
—Virginia Woolf

*People travel to wonder at the height of the mountains,*
*at the huge waves of the seas, at the long course of the rivers,*
*at the vast compass of the ocean, at the circular motion of the*
*stars, and yet they pass by themselves without wondering.*
—St. Augustine

# Focus on Today

*I agree to look within when I react—TODAY.*

*Here are a few simple steps you can take to reduce stressful reactions you have to the way others behave, while getting to know yourself even better. Record your thoughts in your journal.*

1. List three people who tend to trigger strong negative emotions in you when they behave in certain ways, along with their "offending" behavior.
   *Example: HW speaks badly about others behind their backs.*

2. Now it's time to go "soul searching." For each of the behaviors you listed, dig deep until you find something in your own behavior (even if it's from ages ago) that is similar. This may be uncomfortable, but it'll be worth it.
   *Example: I complained to LZ about how HW does that.*

3. The final step is to ask yourself, "How do I feel when I behave that way?" or, "How do I feel about my behaving that way in the past?"
   *Example: I felt vindictive and cruel for talking behind his back.*

4. The next time you notice someone exhibiting this same behavior, ask yourself, "Is my strong emotional reaction tempered now, or even gone altogether?"

You may want to speak to yourself along these lines, "I'll do my best to remember that it's the way I feel about my own behavior that often triggers my disproportionate reaction to similar behaviors in others. It's as though that person holds up a mirror for me to see what I don't like about myself. What I choose to do about my own behavior is not my primary focus right now; my current focus is to disengage from blaming someone else for the way I feel about myself. I will record in my journal the incidents that no longer 'push my buttons.'"

# $\mathcal{A}$GREEMENT FOUR

# I agree to keep doing what works and change what doesn't.

*Insanity is doing the same thing over and over again and expecting different results.*
—Albert Einstein

D o you ever feel imprisoned by your circumstances, wishing you were somewhere else, with someone else, doing something else? What if, instead of feeling stuck, you could set yourself free?

For many years, Glenn gave up time he could have spent in other pursuits to drive our son, Michael, to and from the gym four days a week. Because we lived far away from Michael's fellow gymnasts, we did not have the option to carpool. At times this was a source of frustration for Glenn, so he considered his options:

1. He could drive Michael to the gym and feel victimized by having to do it.
2. He could stop driving Michael to the gym.
3. He could adjust his attitude so that instead of seeing the driving as an interruption in his life, he could look

for what *was* working, such as having precious time alone with his son.

He chose option #3. And when he did, he began noticing more things that were working. Glenn felt good about how he was contributing to all the benefits Michael derived from his gymnastics practice, which included Michael's healthy, strong, flexible body; his positive friendships; practice at goal setting and achieving; building self-esteem and self-confidence; and so much more.

Glenn could easily have said, "I don't *choose* to drive Michael. I *have* to drive him." Had he framed it that way, Glenn likely would not have discovered all the possibilities and rewards available in the situation. But he didn't; he framed it as a positive choice.

The same applied to my carefully chosen words for young Michael when I would tell him, "I am going to work now," rather than the oft-heard lament, "I have to go to work now." Besides teaching our son that we are free to choose rather than being imprisoned by our attitudes, it was also a good reminder for me to check in and be sure that I was choosing work over time with my son at that moment.

This fourth Revolutionary Agreement encourages us to stop whining and start winning; to dig ourselves out of the holes into which we'd fallen; to stop complaining, justifying, or blaming others for situations in our life, and to choose a new path that may work better for all involved.

When considering how to change what doesn't work, Glenn and I have embraced a brilliant question we learned from Master QuantumThink® Coach Alan Collins:[1] *How can we have this work for everyone?*

Imagine if people in power used this simple question to guide their decisions. Here's the good news: every one of us holds power in our own lives, so we can!

## Choose and Re-Choose

People often remain in situations that have long ceased to be productive and, to the contrary, have become an ongoing struggle.

I married young and stayed in my first marriage for eleven years, long after it had stopped working for either of us. If we'd had the habit of honestly reexamining what was and wasn't working, we may have ended our marriage many years earlier—and it would have given us both a new start on life that much sooner.

Having learned what doesn't work, Glenn and I choose to honor and celebrate every precious moment in our lives, rather than committing to a future that is truly unknown.

Our 1984 wedding vows reflected this:

> *"Marriage is not the day of commitment,*
> *but the acknowledgement of it;*
> *It is not a vow to be, but a recognition of what is;*
> *It is not for forever, it is for infinite todays."*

*At the age of 41, I decided to change careers and, coincidentally, so did my husband. He and I both found ourselves in the middle of midlife crises. I was burned out teaching in the public school system, yet I still loved working with kids. My 51-year-old husband was exhausted as an overworked family physician, yet he was still committed to healing. Our relationship was definitely strained because we were redefining our missions in life. At an age when most couples are fairly settled, we were wondering just who and what we wanted to be when we grew up.*

*It was a fearful time and, in hindsight, a blessing in disguise because our communications, out of necessity, reached a depth that ultimately recreated our marriage. In choosing to change what was not working for each of us as individuals we ran the risk of losing each other. What if the choices we made sent each of us in a different direction? We spoke our truths like never before, and we listened with new respect to the challenges and fears the other faced.*

*I found a niche for myself tutoring high school kids in writing. My husband created his own practice, much smaller and more manageable. He is able to get to know his patients, and I am happier knowing I can make a difference with kids on a more intimate level. Together we manifested another mission, our most daring of all: we began the process of adopting a child.*

*—Jean*

What would our lives be like if we reaffirmed our choices daily? We can—and this doesn't apply only to the bigger choices in our lives, like marriage and career; it applies equally to the "little things in life." And sometimes they are not really so little. It is often those simple, daily choices we make that create the life we truly desire—especially the choice of how we spend our time and with whom we spend it.

Friends joined us for dinner one cold winter night. After dinner we settled down in front of the fireplace and someone posed this question, "What would you do if you knew you had only one week left to live?"

What a stimulating question! We took turns responding and noticed that a theme emerged. In our last week of life, each of us in our own way would share what we had learned during our lifetime that might help others.

Our teenage son then changed the game. "What would you do if you knew that everyone on Earth would be gone at the end of that week?" I was stunned. No one left to leave anything to? My first thought was "I'd party hearty!" I didn't know what else to say.

His thought-provoking question woke me up at a deeper level and served as an alarm that randomly sounded, "If I had only one week left to live, would I be doing *this*?"

It became crystal clear that with only one week left I would not be sitting in front of my computer! I would be cherishing every moment with family, friends, and Nature. And for the most part, I now do so.

We are all capable of choosing and re-choosing. Notice the difference between saying, "I *have* to go to work today," and "I *choose* to go to work today." Do you choose it? You did at one time. Does it still serve you? Are you choosing to keep doing what works? Is it time to change what no longer works in your life?

Allow yourself to choose, notice the effects of your choices, and then re-choose based on your experience. "I choose to volunteer for this program." "I choose to work with this company." "I choose and re-choose this marriage." Your choice may also be to change your attitude about what's not working, rather than changing the situation. Only with the freedom to choose do we give ourselves wholly and completely to that which we choose.

## Agreements with the Community

For about eight years, Glenn and I participated in the conception of a Geneva Cohousing Community in Colorado.

Cohousing is a brilliant approach to recreating the best ideals of the villages of yesteryear, when neighbors knew and cared about each other's well-being. While still true in some neighborhoods, it is no longer the norm due to our increasingly mobile society and perceived need for greater privacy. Seeded in Denmark decades ago, cohousing caught on in the US in a huge way in the 1980s, resulting in the development of more than 120 cohousing communities throughout North America.[2]

Cocreating our community provided tremendous opportunities to choose (and re-choose) among different areas of contribution. From locating the cohousing site to developing the land, drafting covenants, doing legal and financial work, designing processes for communication and conflict resolution, creating community activities, designing the community center, and more.

Since we had committed to living the shared mission to *support one another in achieving our life purposes* we had the freedom to choose whatever tasks supported each of us in giving our best. When anyone created a void by opting out of a given work group, someone else with a new level of energy and commitment often filled that void. This never failed to surprise and delight me.

It felt like an "ideal situation." And indeed it was—for a time. But things change.

After eight years of focused effort on initiating our own community, giving a huge amount of our time and energy, we ultimately re-chose: we decided not to continue and, instead, to move to a home elsewhere.

It was a difficult decision and felt at first as confusing and painful as a divorce. Ultimately, moving into an already-established neighborhood in a geographical area more conducive to our growing son's activities proved to better serve our family's needs. And because our cohousing community lived by the Geneva Group Agreements, foundational to the Revolutionary Agreements, our friends supported us in changing what was no longer working for us. We suffered none of the wrath that often erupts when someone on a team has a change of heart or mind.

Some members of Geneva Community seeded another cohousing community near Durango, Colorado. Here's what one of the residents says about the impact of the Agreements on the community she cofounded.

*The Heartwood community in Bayfield, Colorado, started as a dream for a handful of visionaries from Boulder, Colorado. We created a cohousing style "village" placing our 24 homes within a seven-acre area so we could steward the remaining 250 acres. We care for 70 acres of irrigated pasture, pinion, pine, and ponderosa forests with sacred spaces, trails, and gardens. We are from all walks of life, all age groups, single and married, with and without children, and we work both inside and outside the community.*

*Because our community is closely integrated on many levels, it is important that we operate from written agreements to which we all aspire. Our first model was based on the original agreements set forth by the Geneva Group many years ago. As those Agreements have evolved into the Revolutionary Agreements, so have ours evolved to suit our unique needs.*

*New residents undergo training in how to operate with our Agreements. Each meeting starts by reading the Agreements aloud, along with our Vision and Values statements that remind us of why we have chosen to live together in this amazing community.*

*Practicing these Agreements virtually eliminates negative gossip. And the benefits of more compassionate communication and deeper relationships are deeply gratifying.*

*The Agreements are the foundation and the reason our community is thriving. If all communities were to adopt*

> *or adapt these Agreements—families, neighborhoods, businesses, nations (why not?)—the world would be an even more wonderful place to live.*
> *—Gail*

The Heartwood Community Agreements are included in the section on Personalized Agreements on pages 231-232.

## Freedom to Change at Work

With good communication, ample trust, and common goals, people in the workplace can feel free to speak up to change what's not working, and thus serve their businesses' missions at the highest level.

When working with our corporate clients, Glenn and I sometimes instituted weekly half-hour check-ins with each team. First, team members were given "bragging rights," an uplifting way to kick off the check-in by celebrating what was working. Each team member then had an opportunity to speak about something that was *not* working. These items were captured on the left side of a flip chart under the heading "What" and next to two blank columns headed "Who" and "When."

Once all team members had spoken about what was not working that needed their attention, the facilitator would return to the top item and team members would then assign themselves to the items of greatest interest to them. The resulting self-selected teams would each choose a date to implement the change or to meet and determine a strategy for implementing that change.

This highly efficient process cleared out problems before they had time to fester, put solutions in the hands of those most affected by the problems, and gave team members an opportunity to champion changes that resulted in benefits for themselves, their teams, and their organizations.

*Five years with this company and I was seriously wondering how long I would last under the present tumultuous conditions. My challenge was finding a workable solution that would inspire a small, non-performing core organization within our bigger corporation to re-engage and move forward.*

*I met with an internal consultant for some coaching. She gave me a copy of* Revolutionary Agreements *that I read and reread over the weekend. By Monday I was energized and ready to recommit myself to take on the role of facilitating positive changes within this core organization.*

*I put up a poster of the Agreements outside my office and allowed people to notice and ask questions in their own space and time. I worked with one Agreement at a time, watching myself transform as I related to my colleagues in a different way. I discovered the power of* Looking *within when I react and* Listening *with my heart. It was nothing short of amazing. Management noticed a difference in me and their curiosity piqued about these twelve simple guidelines.*

*Soon the management team agreed to engage in a full-day teambuilding workshop facilitated by our consultant. Copies of the Revolutionary Agreements were provided as well as copies of other corporate agreements. We divided into two teams with each team writing their agreements on flip charts. At the end of the working session we came together, combined the charts, and wordsmithed a draft of what became Our Foundation by which we agreed to live and work.*

> *We have been functioning as a cohesive team with our new agreements for seven months now, and to say that this core organization has turned itself around would be an understatement. I look back and remember upper management laughing at my one-year goal strategy. Back then, they did not know about the power of using the Agreements.*
>
> *I can say that I am in love again with my career and assert that the Agreements are the best tools for stress reduction I have ever found.*
> —Dan

This organization's agreements, entitled *Our Foundation*, are included in the Personalized Agreements section, beginning on page 221.

## Everything Used to be Hard

I was raised with a strong work ethic. I believed the harder I worked, the more I deserved the fruits of my labor. So when one of my business partners said, "Our business is so easy, fun, and rewarding!" I did not agree. Fun? Yes. I love working with my friends. Rewarding? Oh, yes. In every way. But easy? No way!

"Really?" I asked. "You think this is easy? "Absolutely," she replied.

We do the same work. She thinks it's easy. I think it's hard. What's going on here?

Perhaps I could have gone to a therapist for a few months and uncovered all the hidden (and not so hidden) messages about the virtues of working hard that I learned from my hard-working parents. Maybe I would have discovered that the harder I worked the more value I thought I was giving to the world. Or that I felt accepted and appreciated based on my sweat factor.

Instead, I asked myself, "Is this working for me? Do I want to move forward feeling like I've worked hard my whole life? Or would I rather feel, like my business partner, that our work was easy?" I chose the latter.

I challenged myself to change what wasn't working—and to change it with ease. Because I had a lifelong habit of making things hard, I had created what Dianne Collins calls a "least action pathway," a well-worn neural route in my brain that keeps me doing the same thing over and over even if I don't like that behavior or its results. In simple terms: I was in a rut. I knew the only way out was to build a new neural pathway to reinforce how easy everything is.

To build my new habit, whenever I became aware of something (*anything*) that was easy, I'd say aloud, "That was easy!" I'd slide the screen door open. Zooooom. "That was easy!" I'd crack the egg in the pan and it would land perfectly whole. "That was easy!"

A friend knew what I was up to and brought me a gift one day: a big red button with the word EASY on top. She said, "Push it." Oh my gosh! A man's deep voice resounded, "THAT was easy!" Now there were two of us to reinforce the new habit I was building.[3]

After just a week or so of noticing all of the many easy things, life actually seemed easier. Could it be that simple? Yes! In fact, changing this lifelong pattern with relative ease continues to serve as an important example for other things I choose to change.

Is there anything in your life that isn't working for you? Perhaps something you would like to be easier? What if it were as simple as changing your mind?

This Agreement is as important for mundane, everyday actions as it is for the greater aspects of our lives. All the little frustrations caused by what's not working can quickly add up to stifle our creativity, productivity, and contributions in the world.

When a situation begins to no longer work, we tend to let it build up and become a drama—the drama of the hopeless situation. Once we reach the point where we know something isn't working, it makes so much more sense to stop, identify it, and take steps to change it—by changing either what we do or how we feel about it.

## What's Working? What's Not?

Where do you experience drama, angst, or strain in your everyday life? Ask yourself, "Is there something that isn't working here? What would happen if I changed what isn't working?" If you like the answer, then you might ask yourself, "Well, what am I waiting for?" (Does waiting work for you?)

Consider making a list of ten things that are working for you and ten things that are not. Listing those things that *are* working for you is just as important as listing those that aren't, so that when you start eliminating or changing what *isn't* working, you don't throw out the baby with the bathwater.

Here's my list for today:

## Ten Things That Are Working For Me
*(in no particular order)*

1. Living where I can walk outside into Nature every morning.
2. Warm climates.
3. Having a loving, supportive husband.
4. QuantumThinking.
5. Eating healthy food.
6. Exercising daily.
7. Sharing the Revolutionary Agreements through Glenn's and my relationship workshops.
8. Loving, respectful relationship with my son.

9. Getting to bed by 10 p.m. so I'm up to enjoy sunrise.
10. Peace of mind from the great care my mom is getting.

## Ten Things That Are *Not* Working For Me
*(in no particular order)*

1. Occasionally eating wheat or sugar.
2. Glenn's love of socializing by dining out.
3. Not enough focused time to write this book!
4. Back-to-back company that reduces much-loved quiet time.
5. Going to bed alone because Glenn stays up later.
6. The awkward stages of growing my hair longer.
7. Trying to come up with ten meaningful things that are not working!

Now I can get to work. As I study these lists, I see right away that I have a "loving, supportive husband" whom I want to *keep*. My eye quickly catches #5 on my "Not Working" list: "Going to bed alone because Glenn stays up later."

How interesting! In the first edition of this book written ten years ago, the first item on my "Not Working" list was "Going to bed too late and joining an already-sleeping husband." My, how times have changed! However, regardless of who is heading to bed first, the issue remains the same. At the end of the day, I want to be near my darling husband.

I have been working to change this. When Glenn is watching a show or reading, I sometimes lay down on the couch near him when I get tired. I figured if I can start a comfortable sleep near him, then later we can both move into the bedroom together. Unfortunately, my solution is not working so well. The couch is too uncomfortable for sleeping.

Three choices occur to me:

1. Continue to feel like a victim.
2. Engage Glenn to think creatively with me about what might work for both of us.
3. Change my attitude about going to bed alone.

As I return to scanning my list, something else jumps out at me—the first item on my "Not Working" list, "Occasionally eating wheat or sugar." Because "Eating healthy food" appeared on my "What is Working" list, I asked myself, "How can I reduce the amount of wheat and sugar I eat?" The answer quickly reveals itself. Carry nuts and dried fruit with me to satisfy my occasional cravings. That was easy!

This simple, powerful process of identifying what is and is not working can be repeated weekly, monthly, or even annually. I encourage you to celebrate what is working in your life and change what is not. Remove the emotional clutter of what's not working. Peace on Earth begins within.

Live a positive life by building on the experiences that feed your soul, nurture your heart, and stimulate your natural intelligence. Eliminate or shift those experiences that drain your energy and light. Life is a grand experience. Let's enjoy the freedom to learn from it, change how we interact with it, and live it with inner joy and peace.

# Words of Wisdom

*"I agree to keep doing what works
and change what doesn't."*

*If you do not change, you can become extinct.*
—Spencer Johnson

*When you blame others,
you give up your power to change.*
—Dr. Robert Anthony

*Change your thoughts and you change your world.*
—Norman Vincent Peale

*True wisdom is less presuming than folly.
The wise man doubteth often, and changeth his mind;
the fool is obstinate, and doubteth not;
he knoweth all things but his own ignorance.*
—Akhenaton

*Things do not change; we change.*
—Henry David Thoreau

*They always say that time changes things,
but you actually have to change them yourself.*
—Andy Warhol

*If you don't like something, change it.
If you can't change it, change your attitude.*
—Maya Angelou

*In a time of drastic change it is the learners who inherit the future. The learned usually find themselves equipped to live in a world that no longer exists.*
—Eric Hoffer

*It's not that some people have willpower and some don't. It's that some people are ready to change and others are not.*
—James Gordon, M.D.

*If you don't change your beliefs, your life will be like this forever. Is that good news?*
—W. Somerset Maugham

*Some people change their ways when they see the light; others when they feel the heat.*
—Caroline Schoeder

*The most powerful agent of growth and transformation is something much more basic than any technique: a change of heart.*
—John Welwood

*To change one's life: Start immediately. Do it flamboyantly. No exceptions.*
—William James

*Only in growth, reform, and change, paradoxically enough, is true security to be found.*
—Anne Morrow Lindbergh

*It is never too late to become what you might have been.*
—George Eliot

# Focus on Today

*I agree to keep doing what works and change what doesn't—TODAY.*

*Here are a few simple steps you can take to minimize struggle and maximize joy in your life by changing what's not working for you. Record your thoughts in your journal.*

1. Begin two lists: "Ten Things That Are Working For Me" and "Ten Things That Are Not Working For Me," and fill them out without thinking about it too much, just writing whatever first comes to mind.

2. Looking at both lists, consider what changes you might choose to make to create greater peace of mind, joy, and fulfillment.

3. Ask yourself, "What are *three positive changes* I can make in items on my "Not Working" list to lighten my life?

4. Then consider, "What one small change am I willing to make *right now* that will support me on my path to inner peace? What am I waiting for? (Does waiting work for me?)"

5. After making the change, reflect upon the results.

# ACCEPTANCE

*God grant me the serenity*
*to accept the things I cannot change,*
*the courage to change the things I can,*
*and the wisdom to know the difference.*
—Reinhold Niebuhr

# ACCEPTANCE

*I AGREE TO:*

*Listen with my heart.*
*Respect our differences.*
*Resolve conflicts directly.*
*Honor our choices.*

The second cluster of Agreements acknowledges and celebrates our differences and can help us graciously navigate the glorious and often bewildering diversity of the human family. Great teachers exemplify acceptance. Jesus taught us to "turn the other cheek." Mahatma Gandhi and Martin Luther King, Jr. inspired us by responding to even the worst kinds of violence with acceptance of others.

Paramahansa Yogananda teaches, "Hating none, giving love to all . . . that is the way to live in this world." Nazi camp survivor and Nobel Peace Prize winner Elie Wiesel offers, "There is divine beauty in learning, just as there is human beauty in tolerance. To learn means to accept the postulate that life did not begin at my birth. Others have been here before me, and I walk in their footsteps."

You don't need to transform into a saint overnight to enjoy the rewards of acceptance. As you start practicing these Agreements, you'll be thrilled to discover you *can* practice them. They are simply new habits of behavior, as doable as drinking an extra glass of water daily. Your rewards will be healthier relationships and greater peace of mind.

# $\mathcal{A}$GREEMENT FIVE

# I agree to listen
# with my heart.

*Listening is a magnetic and strange thing, a creative force.*
*The friends who listen to us are the ones we move*
*toward. When we are listened to, it creates us,*
*makes us unfold and expand.*
—Karl A. Menninger

This Agreement applies the Golden Rule to listening: *Listen to others as you would have them listen to you.* This means listening to more than the words. When we listen with our hearts as well as our minds, we can feel the pulse, the life force that flows through each communication. Conversation may seemingly appear as words strung together, but it far more than that.

## Face Value

You might ask, "Wouldn't it be easier to simply accept what people say at face value?" Well, yes and no. In fact, the expression "face value" is instructive here—because the *value* of someone's face is often significantly more than the value of his or her *words*.

The face (along with the breath, position of the arms, posture of the body, and other nonverbal cues) can provide keys to the emotions or intentions behind the words. Studies have shown that the words we speak comprise far less of our total communication than we may think. People pick up a great deal of what they "hear" from us, consciously or not, from all our other cues and expressions. Peter Drucker offers, "The most important thing in communication is hearing what isn't said."

Does this mean we should ignore people's words and make up our own assumptions about what they're really saying? Absolutely not. This isn't about attempting to be a mind reader, which often just further muddies communication with its assumptions.

When I get the feeling that the person speaking means something different than the words I'm hearing, I simply ask for clarification. This might sound like, "I hear you saying [whatever they're saying], yet I feel some tension. Is there anything else you want to say about this?" Often simply repeating back what I've heard is enough to prompt the other person to clarify the meaning or intention.

In fact, I've found that when I listen carefully from my heart and reflect back what I'm hearing, the speaker may discover they were not actually speaking their truth after all. Being listened to with compassion can be a vital gateway for them to discover and then articulate what lays beneath the surface for them—their own precious truth. This reinforces the potent cycle of conscious communication.

## Listening Doesn't Mean Problem Solving

Stephen R. Covey has observed, "Most people do not listen with the intent to understand; they listen with the intent to reply."

I have found it difficult to listen respectfully when I'm thinking, "You're wrong and I'm right," or, "I remember a time when that happened to me," or even, "What can I do to help you?"

That last train of thought prevented me from truly listening to my mother for many years. Every time my mother complained to me about something during one of our long distance phone conversations, I would immediately jump into problem-solving mode. But then, after I had (to my mind, at least) effectively resolved her situation, she would come back with a ready reason why my solution wouldn't work. We could easily go back and forth like this, me offering solutions and her rejecting them, until it escalated into a bona fide shouting match.

Mom: "I have no milk in the house."

Me: "Why not?"

Mom: "My foot's been hurting too much to go to the store."

Me: "Have you asked one of your friends or neighbors to pick up some milk for you the next time they go?"

Mom: "Oh, I wouldn't bother them. Everyone has their own problems."

Me: "What about services? There must be 'helper' kinds of services in your area. Why don't you call the administration building and see who they recommend?"

Mom: "They won't know."

Me: "Then why don't you look it up in the phone book? Let's see, perhaps you could look under . . ."

Mom: "I'm not going to have just *anyone* come into my home!"

Me: "Arghhhhhh!"

Eventually I learned to listen—*really listen*—and to stop using what she was saying as a springboard for my own need to know better, to be right, to be an all-knowing Protector Supreme. Once I listened with my heart, what I began to hear was a woman who chooses her condition in life, just like the rest of us, and someone who is quite capable even if she is occasionally drawn to act or speak as though she were not.

Then (and *only* then) did I realize that my mother rarely was asking me to help her *resolve* her problems. She just wanted to speak about them, to give them voice. She wanted to be heard, that's all.

From the moment I finally understood this, our relationship blossomed. Mom could say whatever she wanted to, and I no longer got hooked into feeling I was a bad daughter if I couldn't fix her problems. I was off the hook, no longer struggling to come up with the answers. I could see her (and *hear* her) as capable of resolving her own problems—if indeed she even perceived them as problems. My listening without judgment results in her feeling heard. Our conversations nearly always end in the most loving, empowering ways.

Now the phone conversation above might sound more like this:

Mom: "I have no milk in the house."

Me: "Gee, that's too bad. What's going on?"

Mom: "My foot's really been bothering me. I just don't think I can walk around the store on it."

Me: "Gosh, Mom, that must be really hard for you. What are you going to do?"

Mom: "I don't know. I see the doctor again on Tuesday. Maybe he'll have an idea. In the meantime, I'll just have to do without the milk."

Me: "That's too bad." [Time to change the subject.]

The simple act of listening with my heart opens my heart to experience empathy and expands my capacity for non-judgment. Peace on Earth does begin at home!

*When Dad was recently hospitalized, I had an opportunity to see the dynamics of his behavior through more mature eyes. Visiting him in the hospital and listening to him with an open heart, I could see for the first time why he was the way he was and I was able to let go of the past. I no longer took personally some of his comments and was able to actually love him for who he was.*
*—Linda*

## Wanting to Be Heard

I've learned that good listening often doesn't require a substantial response, only the acknowledgment of listening: "yes," "okay," or "tell me more."

I used to drive home from work with my former husband each day, often tightly wound from a day of feeling responsible for a multi-million dollar program and the forty people on my team. Just like my mother (isn't *that* interesting?), I would complain and complain. My husband would respond to me in precisely the same way that I used to respond to my mother (isn't *that also* interesting?). Hardly letting me finish a sentence, he would jump right into solving my problems, brandishing his natural protector's sword and ready to *handle* this situation.

I would get furious—and he would be baffled. What did he do wrong? After all, he'd just jumped to my rescue! What he didn't understand was that all I wanted was to unload and receive emotional support for my feelings, not intellectual or logistical support regarding the issues at hand. Unfortunately, I didn't understand this either at the time, and it became a constant source of tension between us.

I now know that all I ever wanted (and all my mom ever wanted) was to be heard. Just to speak and have someone listen to me—not to tell me what to do, as though I were incapable of figuring it out myself.

*Normally, I would jump right into other people's challenges and offer up my advice intending to "fix" their problems for them. People expect it of me and I always had more than one solution on the tip of my tongue. Listening deeply was a foreign concept to me. Incorporating the Agreements into my daily life has freed me in ways I did not think possible. Here are a couple of examples.*

*Melanie called. She'd found herself between a rock and a hard place and wanted my advice. Her dilemma revolved around whether she should pay a contractor whom she believed had not done as good a job as was expected. I found myself leaning toward her argument but resisted making a judgment.*

*Instead I listened with my heart. I refrained from giving her advice and gently guided the conversation to a place where Melanie was able to see and choose for herself the best option. She chose to pay the agreed contract, seeing this as a better option than hiring expensive attorneys, spending time and energy she could be using elsewhere and creating a potentially adversarial relationship.*

*Irene called. She was having difficulty making a decision about renting to a physically disabled person. The state has certain legal requirements for landlords around equipping their apartments for renters with handicaps and she was not in a financial position to make those additions and changes. She felt pressured by her own ethics and a moral and compassionate desire to be helpful.*

*Once again I listened with my heart. I did not tell her directly what to do but suggested that she tell her own truth compassionately and trust the outcome. She called the prospective renter and shared honestly her predicament. She later told me that she was pleasantly surprised and relieved when the renter listened with complete understanding placing no blame on her.*

*Why are these stories significant for me? I have changed what doesn't work. I no longer feel the need to carry and solve others' problems; instead, by honoring their choices I encourage access to their own power. As I give the gift of heartfelt listening and love, it brings out the best in all of us.*

*—Joe*

## Letting Go of Being Right

I find that I have plenty of opportunities to practice this Agreement. Just this week, I saw how it transformed a lifetime of "I'm right; you're wrong" tension with my brother.

Stephen and I have many philosophical differences. One of them is in the area of wellness. Having been in the natural health industry for twenty years, I believe in natural remedies and addressing the root causes of discomfort. Stephen has always relied on doctors to provide direction and medicine.

As soon as he arrived at our home in Kauai for a visit, he said, "I'm not feeling well. I have to see a doctor tomorrow." For many years, my immediate response would have been to insist he take the natural immune support products I use. I might have even lectured him about how to take better care of his health. Invariably, he would get irritated with me and repeat his need to see a doctor. We have been known to get into fights over this. Not this time.

This time, I heard him. I heard someone who was concerned about his health and who believed that after seeing a doctor, he would feel better. Listening with my heart opened my heart. I offered to take Stephen to a clinic the next morning. After he saw the doctor, he was visibly relieved. The doctor assured him he didn't have anything serious or contagious, and he gave him three medicines to calm his cough and help him sleep. Stephen was happy and on his way to full recovery.

I realized that listening with my heart was oh-so-much easier than engaging in another stressful and useless "I'm right; you're wrong" battle. There is good reason that the word "hear" is central to the word "heart"!

## Listening as Empowerment

Great emphasis is placed on speaking—from the time our parents are eager to hear our first spoken words through all our formal schooling. Not so of listening. Dr. Carol McCall, founder of the Institute for Global Listening and Communication, devotes her life to helping people learn how to truly listen so that we all can be *heard*. Her years of doctoral research have shown that we are measurably healthier, biologically and physiologically, when we feel heard. [1]

I'll never forget the day my son, Michael, met with the school counselor when the stress of his new school had begun taking a toll on his health. He came home from school and exclaimed, wide-eyed, "I could tell Holly anything—*anything*. And she listened . . . Mom, she listened to *everything*!"

I was delighted that Michael experienced really feeling heard. And I was dismayed that it sounded like a new experience for him! Was I not a good listener? I vowed to practice bringing myself fully to listening. I learned that when my mind was elsewhere, it was wise for me to acknowledge it and say something like, "I want to hear what you have to say, but I'm feeling distracted. Can I finish . . . ? Then I'll be able to listen to you fully."

*Had I agreed to listen with my heart earlier in life, I may have been able to give my daughter what she needed then to feel her daddy's love. Now I consciously invite this agreement to guide me in all that I do and I enjoy the result: fulfilling relationships with family and friends.*
*—Jordan*

Imagine speaking with someone who has his or her complete attention on you—on truly hearing what you are saying. No judgment. No assumptions. Nowhere to go and nothing to say, listening fully—just being there for you.

Conversations can be so much more empowering when listening with your heart. Consider the following two scenarios.

Stephanie walks in the door after a particularly grueling day at work and blurts out, "What an exhausting day!" Tom responds by trying to get to the root of the problem so he can help Stephanie feel better. He fires off one question after another, "What happened? . . . Why didn't you tell him so and so? . . . Why don't you make sure that gets fixed tomorrow?"

Is this helping Stephanie's exhausted state? Or worsening it?

Suppose instead of listening with a problem-solving mind, Tom listened compassionately, with his heart. In this case he might ask, "Would it help for you to talk about it?" And then just listen to her. Stephanie may need to talk it out, or she may just need a hug. By listening with his heart, Tom could then respond appropriately.

Dr. Peter Senge suggests we practice "generative listening." He says, "Generative listening is the art of developing deeper silences in yourself, so you can slow your mind's hearing to your ears' natural speed, and hear beneath the words to their meaning."[2]

Listening is for the other person. It's not about us. Yet when we listen with our heart, it can open our heart to feel even more loving and accepting.

Listening with your heart opens channels for the deepest, most meaningful communications you may ever experience; for friendships that go beyond the usual surface chatter; for teams where the members feel heard and empowered; and for devoted relationships that spread love like ripples in the pond of your life . . . and beyond.

# Words of Wisdom

*"I agree to listen with my heart."*

*In order that all men may be taught to speak truth,*
*it is necessary that likewise all should learn to hear it.*
—Samuel Johnson

*Listening is being able to be changed by the other person.*
—Alan Alda

*You cannot truly listen to anyone and*
*do anything else at the same time.*
—M. Scott Peck

*I know you believe you understand*
*What you think I said,*
*But I am not sure you realize*
*What you heard*
*Is not what I meant.*
—Robert McCloskey

*A good listener is not only popular everywhere,*
*but after a while he gets to know something.*
—Wilson Mizner

*Gentlemen, listen to me slowly.*
—Samuel Goldwyn

*The first duty of love is to listen.*
—Paul Tillich

*So when you are listening to somebody, completely, attentively,*
*then you are listening not only to the words,*
*but also to the feeling of what is being conveyed,*
*to the whole of it, not part of it.*
—Jiddu Krishnamurti

*The more faithfully you listen to the voices within you,*
*the better you will hear what is sounding outside.*
—Dag Hammarskjöld

*Friends are those rare people who ask how we are,*
*and then wait to hear the answer.*
—Ed Cunningham

*Courage is what it takes to stand up and speak;*
*courage is also what it takes to sit down and listen.*
—Winston Churchill

*As I get older, I've learned to listen to people*
*rather than accuse them of things.*
—Po Bronson

*Put your ear down close to your soul and listen hard.*
—Anne Sexton

*To listen fully means to pay close attention to what is being said*
*beneath the words. You listen not only to the 'music,' but to the*
*essence of the person speaking. You listen not only for what*
*someone knows, but for what he or she is.*
—Peter Senge

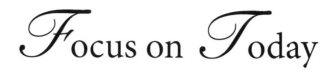

# Focus on Today

*I agree to listen with my heart—TODAY.*

*Here are a few simple ways to improve relationships by listening with your heart. Record your thoughts in your journal.*

1. Becoming aware of when you're not listening with your heart is the first step in changing listening habits. Thinking over recent interactions, ask yourself the following questions:

    a) When was I listening with judgment?
    *Example: I notice I don't even listen to Fred anymore because I'm expecting to hear him whine. Maybe if I genuinely listened occasionally he would feel heard and stop whining.*

    b) When was I analyzing how to help the speaker?
    *Example: Stephanie started complaining again. I couldn't wait to tell her how to fix her problem. I could have just said empathetically, "Gee, that's too bad. I'm sure you'll figure it out." Instead I acted like a know-it-all and didn't allow her to simply vent.*

    c) When was I thinking about what to say next?
    *Example: While Pat was talking, I kept interrupting to say I could relate to what she was saying because of similar situations in my life. This was unnecessary, self-centered, and broke her train of thought.*

2.  How do you choose to improve your ability to listen with your heart today?

    *Example: By quieting my mind when listening to my brother, allowing him to be fully heard without judging or attempting to fix the problem (or him!).*

# $\mathscr{A}$GREEMENT SIX

# I agree to respect our differences.

*If we cannot end now our differences,*
*at least we can help make the world safe for diversity.*
—John F. Kennedy

A s we grow up and venture beyond the confines of our homes and neighborhoods, a world of exquisite diversity greets us. We each add our unique contributions to the rich tapestry of life's magnificent discoveries, innovations, and works—all created by the weaving of our differences.

What would life be like if one particular set of thoughts or one specific way of doing things were considered the only way? The answer seems obvious. Without different ideas, creativity would be stifled. Without fresh perspectives, problems might never be solved. Without different styles and approaches, the world would be a dreary, stultifying place with a multitude of undone tasks, unsolved problems, and uninspired, unengaged people.

While this feels quite apparent as I write this, there have been plenty of times in my life when I earnestly believed that if everyone simply did it *my* way, life would be much better.

As parents, we'd love our kids to do it our way. As spouses, we want our partner to squeeze the toothpaste tube the same way we do. It's only natural to have the tendency to want people to do it our way. Collectively, what would happen if we all somehow got our wishes? Disaster!

This Agreement applies just as importantly to mundane differences as it does to the deep-seated philosophical, religious, and political disagreements that underlie wars.

The distinctions between varying genders, races, cultures, political alignments, and religious beliefs can feel highly charged. Learning to respect them (even just to accept them) allows us to access phenomenal possibilities and creativity.

But smaller things can be equally important. Some might say they are even *more* important because they figure into our lives at every moment. Our lives are created not predominately in great dramatic strides, but in the ways we choose to live one minute at a time, day by day.

> *This Agreement helped me immensely in healing my relationship with my only sibling, my older sister. During early childhood, we often had fun and, like all siblings, conflict. I viewed my sister as the powerful one, both physically and mentally; I often felt weak and disempowered. To further strain our tenuous relationship, as we grew older, we found ourselves on opposing sides of the political fence. "Respecting our Differences" was vital to healing our relationship. The key was to feel comfortable with who I am while allowing her to be herself.*
> —*Linda*

## Common Goals, Different Paths

The original Geneva Group Agreement behind "Respect our Differences" is, "I agree to come from a sense of cooperation and caring in my interactions with others, and from an understanding that goals are often the same even though methods for achieving them may differ." Nowhere has this played a greater role in my life than in the care of my aging mother.

My brother Stephen and I used to disagree about almost everything. In 2012, our disagreement revolved around the life (and potentially imminent death) of our mother.

While talking with mom by phone, I could tell something was wrong. She was laboring to catch her breath. I ordered blood tests, which revealed she was severely anemic. What could be the cause of this? I was told the most likely culprit was internal bleeding. She needed to go to the hospital, but she refused.

Stephen and I spoke long distance. I was supportive of mom's desire to stay away from hospitals because of their reputation for increasing health risks. Also, mom said that at her age (then 94), she wasn't likely to take any action to repair the cause of internal bleeding if that was the issue. So why bother? Mom attributed her healthy life, in part, to staying away from doctors and hospitals. I certainly did not want mom's last days to be in an environment of which she was deathly afraid. I told my brother I didn't want mom going to the hospital.

Stephen strongly disagreed. Unlike mom, he always sought doctors' advice and never hesitated to go to the ER if faced with a health issue. He insisted that she go to the hospital immediately.

We hung in there with each other, remembering we shared the goal to support mom in having the highest possible quality of life for the longest possible time. I shared my concerns about mom going to the hospital. Stephen shared his concerns about her *not* going. We found common ground—mom would go for transfusions to ease the congestive heart failure she was experiencing from her low blood volume. We would not allow any invasive procedures to identify the cause of her blood loss, honoring her request for no surgery at her age. We would simply wait and see if she resumed her usual good energy after the transfusions.

Thank goodness for being able to practice this Agreement! Even though we fundamentally differ on our use of medical care, we found common ground because our goal was the same. Because of this, mom returned to her active life three days after entering the hospital. Three years later, she is still living independently and with good health in her retirement community.

## Doing and Being

In our early days of business consulting together, I often was bothered by Glenn's approach to work. I loved to be highly productive, to produce *things*. Glenn was highly creative; he loved to gestate *ideas*. It seemed to me that I was always working—creating job aids, procedural manuals, consumer guides, etc. I was busy, busy, busy, while Glenn was walking around our client's workplace, schmoozing with the employees and top executives. Why was I doing all the work? It made me furious.

But what was Glenn really up to? Keeping in mind our common goal—*to help increase our client's productivity*—he was being observant. Every few weeks, after noticing, listening, and considering, his creative mind, unburdened by the busyness of my producing mind, might come up with a million-dollar idea—an idea simple for our client to implement while also paying off in increased productivity and bottom-line profits.

It took time for me to learn one of life's most important lessons: *each of us has something to contribute*. It isn't always immediately evident what that "something" is, but if we respect our differences and recognize that our goals are often the same even when our methods for achieving them may differ, we will be far more likely to recognize those contributions.

When I began to grasp the contributions Glenn was making and see how they complemented the work I was doing, this Agreement took on new meaning for me. I also began to see my coworkers in a new light, looking for their gifts rather than being critical of their approaches when they differed from mine. I began to understand more deeply that there is more than one way to reach the same goal, and a diversity of approaches may be even more productive.

## Unity in Diversity

We see examples of this in every aspect of life. Look at any good sports team. It takes each player performing different yet complementary roles to get the ball across the goal line.

Think of the goals we typically share with our neighbors in our communities. To feel safe and secure. To feel loved and accepted. To have freedom of choice. Do we all accomplish these goals in the same way? Of course not. For example, I believe that the best way to be safe is to get to know my neighbors well, while others feel safe only when they have loaded guns in their homes. Although this would not be my choice, I have learned to respect it as theirs. My interactions with family members and coworkers taught me that a posture of "I'm right; you're wrong" does nothing towards meeting shared goals.

Many of us work in environments with stated common goals. Perhaps it's an organizational mission and objectives for accomplishing them. Yet despite a supposedly shared mission, it sometimes can feel as if our coworkers and we are from different planets! Putting this Agreement into practice in the workplace allows us to tap the strength that comes from seeing the unity in diversity.

It takes new ideas and innovations to evolve a brand and organization. If I express antagonism rather than cooperation on my work team, I short-circuit the path to our common goal. Similarly, if I keep new ideas to myself (for the sake of "maintaining harmony"), I eliminate our chances for the synergy of teamwork to produce extraordinary results.

## Different Personalities

While the workplace can provide ample opportunities to practice this Agreement, there is much truth in what Dorothy said in *The Wizard of Oz*, "There's no place like home."

In our homes, we may share the common goal of a loving, peaceful environment. But for this to be a reality, we must find ways for each person to meet his or her own needs while not infringing on those of others.

Understanding that each of us functions differently—with varying personalities, styles, needs, and desires—is essential. For example, having plenty of privacy may be important to one family member, while another may thrive more on social interaction. The key is to learn how to nurture ourselves while supporting other members of our households to do the same. This goes a long way to help eliminate the "victim syndrome" we so often find in our homes.

For years, Glenn and I were happily at each other's sides for work and play. Now I find that socializing at the level that stimulates Glenn can exhaust me. We are learning how to support one another in getting what we each need in this new stage of life without compromising our marriage. For example, Glenn is supportive of me traveling by myself to study with my Tai Ji teacher for two or three consecutive weeks each year. He invites a buddy of his to fly in and visit during those times so he can socialize to his heart's content.

I support Glenn by attending some social events I wouldn't choose to go to if it weren't for his request that I accompany him. At those events, Glenn enjoys moving around to connect with many people, while I typically find one friend with whom I'm happy to go off into a corner and enjoy an intimate conversation.

When I told a friend I was feeling uncomfortable with my recent desire to be alone more, she suggested I read the book, *Quiet: The Power of Introverts in a World That Can't Stop Talking.*[1] I am familiar with a "world that can't stop talking." I helped to create it! At this time in my life, however, I'm craving more quiet time. The book *Quiet* is helping me understand that how I feel is normal. Yet knowing this doesn't automatically create the time and space for me to experience greater solitude. It's up to me to discover the many ways to honor my needs while staying connected to my beloved husband.

## Differing Beliefs

In the grand scheme of things, nowhere is it more important to respect differences than when it comes to our deepest beliefs.

For example, the words and ways in which we choose to experience our spirituality are multitudinous. My desire to respect different beliefs has provided many opportunities for me to understand, appreciate, and strengthen my own relationship to the Source of Life.

Years ago I was involved in a company in which colleagues proselytized and prayed for me often. For someone else, this may have felt good. But for me, with my culturally Jewish childhood and my nonreligious adulthood, I felt judged, excluded, and annoyed. From a professional perspective, I was extremely uncomfortable with the religious fervor these evangelists expressed whenever they took the stage at a public or business event.

After a series of communications with one of my mentors about my frustration with this situation, he wrote, "When does your judgment about their judgment become intolerance?" That stopped me in my tracks. After all, one-third of my first edition of *Revolutionary Agreements* is about being nonjudgmental!

I stopped resisting. I opened to learning more about these coworkers' beliefs. Once I did so, I began to see my colleagues as loving, caring people on a mission they believed would help as many people as possible get to life everlasting in a place they call Heaven. I realized their actions came from a deeply compassionate place. With my new perspective, I found myself more loving and accepting of who they are, and my angst dissolved.

We have seen what thousands of years of "I'm right; you're wrong" have accomplished. How many people have been killed for their beliefs? How many are being killed today? Isn't it time that we citizens of the world evolve from killing each other for our beliefs to respecting our differences?

Imagine if our children, instead of saying to each other, "You talk funny," or, "You're stupid," learned to say thoughtfully, "That's a different way of thinking about that."

Children tend to learn prejudice from those closest to them—from their families, friends, teachers, coaches—as well as from the collective societal thinking (social consciousness) to which we all contribute. We all can be more mindful of how we speak to and about others—and how we can more *positively* influence our children and communities at large.

I remember remarking to a friend one day after having her daughter in my car, "Your daughter sure likes to talk badly about other children." She replied, "I guess she learns that from me. I have a tendency to complain in front of her about people I think are jerks." I was struck by the woman's honesty and self-awareness. Many people are as unaware of the judgments they carry (and broadcast) as of the air they breathe.

Since he was six years old, I have told our son that one of the really cool things about being human is that we can believe whatever we choose. So why not choose to believe in those things that are positive and loving, those things that foster the betterment of humanity and the world? When sharing the idea that everyone can believe whatever they want, I would explain that some people choose to believe that *their* belief is the *only* truth . . . and that's okay, too, because that's *their* belief.

*The problem with any agreement is that it is easier to say yes with our minds than to actually do. The concept of respecting differences is obviously a good idea. But what happens when we try to put it into practice?*

*When talking with one of my daughters one day, she shared how she felt about her own daughter when she was being sassy and showing an attitude.*

*"Ah yes," I said. "You sent me to my room in tears a few times."*

*I got to wondering whether it would have helped if I'd had the Agreement to respect differences thirty years ago.*

*Marian Head [in her book,* Revolutionary Agreements*] suggests that we ask ourselves the question, "Who are those people in my life with whom I have the most difficulty?" Then we should write down what it is that bugs us about them.*

*Then, Marian says, for every reason you list about why someone bugs you, try to find a positive aspect of that same behavior. We are to ask ourselves, "How can I change my attitude from disdain to appreciation?"*

*With my daughter I could have written, "My daughter is blunt and forceful." The positive aspect of her behavior is that she is not afraid to speak her mind. She has a strong will and is able to state strong opinions instead of cowering in the corner. Then I could have written, "She likes to argue." The positive is that she can express her thoughts clearly and doesn't mind taking on a challenge.*

*This, Marian says, is a way to soften our response, to release unproductive drama in our life and foster an empowering environment in which people feel free to express their true selves. Think of all the tears and drama I might have avoided if I'd had this understanding back then!*

*Let's try some other examples. A boss is very controlling. He likes things to be his way or the highway. The positive? He gets things done, and he often has a plan that will work.*

*You experience a relative as whining and complaining. The positive? She cares about things, and she wants to see things improved.*

*Frankly, it's really challenging. However, . . . by forcing ourselves to see the positive aspects of an annoying behavior, we can free ourselves from the illusion that the other is wrong and we need to fix or change them.*[2]

*—Martie*

## "Respect" Doesn't Mean "Agree With"

This Agreement is yet another facet of the Golden Rule, "Respect others the way you wish to be respected." But it's important to be very clear about the following distinction. Does "respect" mean "agree with"? Not necessarily.

In the immediate aftermath of 9/11, I witnessed a world coming together in compassion. I thought, "Perhaps this is a turning point for a majority of humanity to feel our connection as one human race." I was deeply disappointed when President Bush decided to use the event to justify invading Iraq.

I view war in a similar way to how I view our "standard of care" for curing certain human illnesses. Even though Nature's bounty, laughter, love, and prayer have been shown to support our inner defense systems' ability to reverse serious illnesses, our medical system still promotes cutting out the problem. I saw this in parallel to then President Bush's decision to cut out the area of "illness" he blamed for 9/11.

While I didn't agree with his rationale for initiating this war, I saw that perhaps President Bush and I have shared desires for personal freedom and peace in our world. I took the opportunity, during that highly charged period, to practice respecting these differences while continuing to speak my truth, with compassion; to make a contribution with my every word and action; and to not give up on something I believe in, while respecting the rights of those who believe differently.

I have recognized that each person I meet adds value to my life—and to life itself. In my younger, ego-strong days, I sometimes acted as if I were an eye cell, for example, believing that my role was the most important one in the body. Then I discovered that all the cells I had been judging because they weren't like me—ears, liver, heart, etc.—also had vital functions to play. I now embrace being a unique part of the more than seven billion parts that make up the body of humanity.

When we release the great burden of judging others (and ourselves), we experience greater peace in our own lives. When enough of us recognize and respect the multifaceted nature of our human race, we advance Peace on Earth.

# Words of Wisdom

*"I agree to respect our differences."*

*Everything we shut our eyes to, everything we run away from,*
*everything we deny, denigrate, or despise, serves to defeat us in*
*the end. What seems nasty, painful, evil, can become a source*
*of beauty, joy, and strength, if faced with an open mind.*
*Every moment is a golden one for him who has the*
*vision to recognize it as such.*
—Henry Miller

*As we grow as unique persons,*
*we learn to respect the uniqueness of others.*
—Robert H. Schuller

*If civilization is to survive, we must cultivate*
*the science of human relationships—*
*the ability of all peoples, of all kinds,*
*to live together and work together,*
*in the same world, at peace.*
—Franklin D. Roosevelt

*Before God we are all equally wise—and equally foolish.*
—Albert Einstein

*It is never too late to give up your prejudices.*
—Henry David Thoreau

*Opinions founded on prejudice are always*
*sustained with the greatest of violence.*
—Francis Jeffrey

*The essence of our effort to see that every child has a chance*
*must be to assure each an equal opportunity,*
*not to become equal, but to become different—*
*to realize whatever unique potential of*
*body, mind, and spirit he or she possesses.*
—John Martin Fischer

*I never meet a ragged boy in the street without feeling that*
*I may owe him a salute, for I know not what possibilities*
*may be buttoned up under his coat.*
— James A. Garfield

*Have a dialogue between the two opposing parts*
*and you will find that they always start out fighting each other*
*until we come to an appreciation of difference . . .*
*a oneness and integration of the two opposing forces.*
*Then the civil war is finished, and your energies are ready*
*for your struggle with the world.*
—Frederick Salomon Perls

*I believe in God, only I spell it Nature.*
—Frank Lloyd Wright

*Believing ourselves to be possessors of absolute truth*
*degrades us: we regard every person whose way of thinking*
*is different from ours as a monster and a threat*
*and by so doing turn our own selves into*
*monsters and threats to our fellows.*
—Octavio Paz

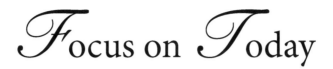

# Focus on Today

*I agree to respect our differences—TODAY.*

*Here are two simple steps to begin releasing unproductive drama in your life and fostering an empowering environment in which people feel free to express their true Selves. Record your thoughts in your journal.*

1. Who are the people in your life with whom you have the most difficulty? And what is it that bugs you about him or her?
   *Example: MM, because of his know-it-all attitude.*

2. Now ask yourself, "For every reason I listed above about what bugs me, what might be a positive aspect of that same behavior? And how can I change my attitude from disdain to appreciation?
   *Example: The truth is, MM actually does know a lot. He could be a good resource. And what I can appreciate about him is that he freely and unselfishly shares what he knows.*

# $\mathcal{A}$GREEMENT SEVEN

# I agree to resolve conflicts directly.

*It's not a problem that we have a problem.*
*It's a problem if we don't deal with the problem.*
—Mary Kay Utecht

Living in a world of diversity, it is inevitable that conflicts occur. "Respecting our differences" doesn't mean ignoring or glossing over conflicts. On the contrary, it means treating the conflicts with respect as well. This Agreement asks us to handle problems directly, which means with speed and compassion and always—*always*—by speaking directly with the person with whom we have the problem.

Why do we so often tend not to do this? Before I experienced the peace of mind that results from practicing this Agreement, I used to do anything I could to avoid confrontation. If I got provoked, I would first solidify my position (proving I was right) by making the rounds and telling "my side" of the issue to people I trusted to build up support for my case. There's strength in numbers, right?

Wrong. In fact, when it comes to resolving conflict, I've learned that greater numbers only compound the problem. In fact, when it comes to resolving conflict, there is often *weakness* in numbers. Years of practicing this Agreement have taught me that strength lies in direct communication, with compassion, as soon as possible. Going directly to speak with the person with whom I can resolve the conflict minimizes unnecessary drama and stress.

> *I was reared in an environment in which my parents' authority was the rule. There was not much encouragement for the expression of my thoughts and feelings. I tended to be silent and avoid conflict in order to not rock the boat.*
>
> *Recently, I put the Agreements to the test by speaking my truth to someone with whom I had an issue but was uncomfortable addressing it. Speaking my truth with the element of compassion added the integrity that allows this process to work even when both parties do not agree.*
>
> *The result: freedom. I now allow myself the freedom to speak, respecting both myself and the other person. I speak confidently about my feelings without fearing a reaction and issues are no longer bottled up inside me. The Agreements reaffirm that I have many options on how I handle conflict. I have unlimited choices, I don't take things personally, and I allow myself respect while offering that same opportunity to others.*
>
> *I feel much lighter and notice daily how the Agreements integrate into my life. In my personal copy of* Revolutionary Agreements, *I note where an Agreement is mentioned in the Bible. For instance, Matthew 18:15 describes "Resolve conflicts directly" with these words, "If your brother sins against you, go and tell him his fault, between you and him alone."*
>
> *—Suzy*

I still step outside this Agreement from time to time. When that happens, when I catch myself complaining about someone who is not present, I am moved to go clean it up immediately. I may call the person I spoke with and say, "I really shouldn't have talked to you about Person X. I'm going to be calling that person directly, and I hope you'll do me the favor of not passing on what I said to anybody else." Then I go speak directly to the person who is at the source of my issue.

I've said that embracing these Agreements and living a positive life takes courage. Of all the Agreements, this one can feel like it takes the most courage of all. And, as with all sincere acts of courage, the rewards are well worth it.

## Dismantling the Rumor Mill

The workplace is a notorious hotbed for gossip, yet interestingly, I've found this Agreement tends to be welcomed in the workplace with tremendous enthusiasm. When offered a way to dismantle the fickle and destructive institution of the rumor mill by adopting a more constructive way to behave, people embrace it with open arms.

The next time you hear an upsetting rumor at work, what if instead of passing on the bad news and your upset feelings to your coworkers, you instead went directly and immediately to the source of the issue and said, "I just heard . . . and wanted to know whether or not it's true."

I have done this dozens of times. Sometimes I hear the response, "No, it's certainly *not* true," and then have the delight of sharing the good news with my coworkers. Sometimes I will learn that yes, in fact, the rumor is true. In either case, I am always happy to return my attention to my work more quickly than if the drama of a festering rumor were to continue.

I heard once through the grapevine that "Jack," a friend and member of my network marketing organization, had begun working for a different (and competing) company. My first angry impulse was to call the key people in our organization up and down the line, as well as key people at the corporate office, and tell everyone of Jack's traitorous acts. In my shocked disbelief, my mind scrambled to come up with a plan for researching the competing company so we could map out a defensive strategy for keeping Jack's people from leaving our company and joining the new one with which he had purportedly aligned himself.

Luckily for all involved, the essence of this Agreement kicked in before I took any action.

Instead, I sent Jack an email, "I just heard that you were leading a training call for another network marketing company. Can you enlighten me?" He wrote back, "I have been hired by this new network marketing company to teach their associates my cold-calling techniques. I am getting paid to do this, and yes, they have also given me a position in their network as part of my compensation. However, other than the teaching I've been hired to do, I am pursuing no other income from this new company. My allegiance always has been and always will be with the company we both love."

It took only minutes to go to the source and resolve this issue to my complete satisfaction. Can you imagine how long it would have taken me to clean up the damage I could have caused had I passed on the rumor that Jack had abandoned ship?

*In my landscaping business I hire gardeners and outside contractors. One time I hired a gardener whose goal was to start her own business someday. To my dismay, I discovered that this woman was gardening for me with one hand and repeatedly using her cell phone with the other. I approached her, feeling clear and nonjudgmental, and*

130

*said, "While you work for me I request your commitment to be focused on this job and catch up on your personal business at lunch or breaks." Apparently, this was just what she needed to hear to move her to a decision to step out and start her own business. Now she has her own employee challenges, and she hires me to consult with her on landscaping.*

*Great relationships make successful businesses, and great relationships are based on the trust that comes from resolving conflicts directly.*

*—Dorothy*

## The Camel and the Straw

In this Agreement, the word "directly" has two meanings: it means going straight to the person involved and speaking with him or her—and it also means *as soon as possible*. One of the keys to successful problem-solving is timing, and that applies here.

We don't want to engage a contributor to a problem until we are calm enough to listen with our heart, yet at the same time, we also don't want to wait too long to deal with it.

Here's an analogy that has helped me remember to resolve problems as quickly as possible.

Every time something upsets you, imagine that you are taking a rock and dropping it into a pack that you wear on your back at all times. Small upsets may be only small rocks ("No big deal . . ."), but after years of accumulating them, that pack can get pretty heavy. Once you reach a certain point, adding even one more rock, no matter how small—even a pebble—can finally throw you completely off balance.

That pebble is what people call "the straw that broke the camel's back."

Have you ever said something you thought was minor, yet the person you said it to responded with a *major* response, one that seemed way out of proportion to your slight transgression? Even if it seemed like a pebble to you, what you gave that person may well have been more than their heavy backpack could carry . . . the last straw.

We may think (as I have many times), "This is so small, so insignificant—it's not worth the trouble to bring it up and hash it over again." Perhaps not. But by not resolving it at the earliest opportunity, we've chosen to add a rock or two to the accumulation of emotional baggage in our lifelong collection.

*In our office there's a coworker I thought of as "The Office Bully." He could be verbally abusive and his temper rose at the slightest provocation. This would resurrect my old fears and memories of the abuse I suffered at the hands of my father and I would immediately retreat.*

*I never had the courage to deal with it directly until one night when he called, obviously drunk, and shouted all sorts of abuse and accusations at me for no valid reason. Rather than react and take it personally, I decided to step up and resolve this conflict directly.*

*I said, "I don't deserve this kind of abuse and I won't talk to you while you're drunk. When you're sober and calm and want to talk rationally, then you can call me."*

*I was pleasantly surprised when the man did contact me the next day and apologized for being drunk and abusive. I could have let it go at that, but I decided it was time to speak my truth if we were to have a decent working relationship. I discussed honestly and calmly what wasn't working in the office and our business relationship and suggested some ways we could change it for the better.*

*He actually listened and thanked me for sharing. Our relationship is much more constructive and, even though we do not always agree, we have created greater respect for each other's point of view.*
—Bill

## The Power of Multiple Agreements

The practice of any one Agreement leads naturally to the others. This is especially obvious with this Agreement.

Before going to speak with the person to *resolve the conflict directly*, stop and *look within at your reaction*. Examining your own reactions and emotional responses to the situation first can go a long way to removing any excessive emotional charge on the issue for you, and you may find yourself in a far better position to present the issue clearly and dispassionately. Sometimes you'll find that once you look within at your reaction, the issue is no longer with the other, but rather is something unresolved within yourself.

When you do speak with the person, you'll want to *speak your truth, with compassion*. It is a wonderful feeling to have the habit of asking ourselves, when faced with an emotional issue, "How can I speak my truth with compassion in this moment?" rather than simply reacting from a place of, "All right. How can I unload a lifetime of rocks right now?"

And as you problem-solve together, you'll be *listening with your heart*.

When there's a conflict, you can use not one, not two, but four of these Revolutionary Agreements to transform the situation.

*I use two sets of agreements for my retreats: one for staff (coaches, facilitators, and administration) and one for my clients to use as a working model to help develop their own agreements. Our agreements have made working together so much easier, with less struggle and difficulty among staff or with clients. In fact, using the agreements saved us from losing a retreat participant.*

*One of our participants was experiencing a personal challenge with a particular facilitator. She was very frustrated and came to me to voice her complaint. I listened deeply and compassionately, allowing her to vent and dispel the heat from her argument. I drew her attention to the agreements she willingly signed at the beginning of the retreat. Eventually, she was ready to participate again and practice resolving her conflict directly (with the facilitator) by speaking her truth compassionately. The facilitator drew upon the agreements about listening deeply and honoring differences. As a result, there was no collusiveness or divisiveness, everything lightened up and our participant remained to finish the retreat. It was quite an empowering learning for all involved.*

*—Melisa*

## Under One Roof

This Agreement may be the reason our family was able to live under the same roof for so many years with my best friend, Gail, and her husband, Gregory. We did this initially for purely economic reasons. Both couples traveled extensively for our work, and this arrangement afforded us all a magnificent home in the mountains to return to between trips. Soon, though, we came to enjoy the camaraderie of built-in neighbors and friends.

Quite a few people were surprised (some might have said "amazed") that we were able to share our home for thirteen years and still successfully remain friends. How did we create a harmonious environment for four—and eventually, with the addition of our son, Michael—for five? After all, doesn't "familiarity breed contempt"?

The answer was simply that to the best of our abilities, we lived by these Agreements—and this particular Agreement was the cornerstone. Whenever the slightest issue or potential bone of contention arose, we would address it in the moment, or at least as soon as possible once upset feelings had a chance to calm down. We didn't gossip. We didn't take sides. We didn't complain to someone else about an issue with another. We took our issues directly to the person or persons with whom we could resolve it—*always*.[1]

*I used to expect my husband to "read my feelings." I was more of a "people pleaser" and preferred to drop hints about what I wanted and rarely spoke directly to the issue. Both my husband and I came from similar backgrounds where showing anger or displeasure meant, "You don't love me." It took time to make the Agreement "Resolve Conflicts Directly" a consistent component to our relationship and the results are well worth it.*

*Our marriage is stronger and more honest. Our relationship not only survives, it thrives because our communications are direct, truthful, and respectful of each other's point of view.*

*—Sigrid*

## How to Broach the Issue

Because it can be difficult to begin the communication, I have learned some starter phrases that work for me, regardless of the issue. Feel free to use one or more of them.

"Something doesn't feel right."

"Why did you say that to me? That didn't feel good."

"Something just happened that doesn't feel good to me."

"This isn't working for me."

In our situation with Gail, Gregory, Glenn, and me all living under one roof, here is the kind of exchange we typically found ourselves having in the spirit of this Agreement: "Marian—what can we do about your leaving the dishes in the sink? We've talked about this before, but you keep slipping into old habits." As the reigning drama queen of our household, I might groan, "Ahh . . . I've been *so* busy today!" The silence would let me know that Gregory wasn't accepting the invitation to join my pity party. With no other way out, I would move to resolution, "I'll take care of it in about an hour, when I finish what I'm doing, okay? And I'll try to stay on top of it in the future."

By being vulnerable, not having the answers, not controlling the situation, but simply stating, "Something isn't working here," we often found we could open the door to collaboration and ease in resolving potentially uncomfortable situations.

*I own a rental property on the river in Estes Park, Colorado. When it is not rented I like to go there myself to enjoy the quiet beauty of the surroundings. Recently I invited a friend to join me for a weekend and we went up anticipating quiet walks, reading, and good conversation. When I arrived I noticed that the owners of the property next door had a new tenant. There were lots of cars parked outside and it appeared there was a party in progress.*

The evening wore on and instead of winding down, the party got even rowdier. When we retired for the night, we hoped the sounds of the river might drown out the noise next door. I chose the bedroom closest to the house next door hoping that my friend would have a better chance at quiet in the other room. At 2 a.m. I awakened to party noise.

The next morning I asked my friend how she slept and she remarked, "I was fine until about 2 a.m. when I heard the party going on next door." That did it. I decided I would call the owners of that house and let them know just what kind of tenant they had and the disturbance they were making. After all, I had my future tenants to think of and it could affect my rental business.

Ironically, I had just read Revolutionary Agreements, which I had shared with my friend over the weekend. Suddenly, the agreement, "I agree to resolve conflicts directly," popped into my head. Hmmm. This was my opportunity. I walked next door, rang the doorbell and waited until a young man answered. He was slightly disheveled and looked like he'd been up all night, which was not surprising. I spoke my truth and asked, "Is this what I can expect every night?" He was most apologetic and replied that this was an unusual occurrence. They were celebrating the birthdays of three people and chose to have one big party. He assured me it would not happen again.

The agreements are valuable because they bring so many things into conscious awareness. Through the use of just one agreement, I was able to resolve this conflict directly, easily, and amicably for both parties without unnecessarily involving the owners. I realized how often

> *we tell others instead of speaking directly to those with whom
> we can resolve our issues and am grateful for this positive
> experience of putting the Revolutionary Agreements into
> action.*
>    —*Kathy*

## What If They Come to Me?

This Agreement takes on an interestingly different hue in cases where someone else comes to you with a complaint, rather than taking it to the person it involves. You may not want to refuse to hear your friend or coworker, but you also don't want to support third-party, indirect communication. What can you do?

My first response would be to ask compassionately, "Is this something you'd like to resolve?" Regardless of whether their answer is yes or no, I would gently redirect them to speak with the person with whom they can resolve the issue. "I am not the best person to help you. The person you have the issue with is really the only one who can help you. Why don't you invite him or her to resolve this together in a way that works for both of you?"

Occasionally, we may find it helpful to seek counsel from a coach, spiritual leader, or trusted friend (especially trusted not to share any details with others). That advisor may be able to help us clarify our own motivations and guide us on how to communicate our upsets in a mature way.

Perhaps my most significant experience with this Agreement was when I had a conflict with my longtime friend and business partner, Gail. Together we had created a hugely successful network marketing business and were both happily focused on other passions, supported by the residual income we had created. Then one day she told me that she wanted to refocus on growing our networking business. She said that if I didn't partner with her again, she would reduce the percentage of income I would be receiving. I was stunned.

We made a date to get together to discuss this. On my drive to her house, I angrily reviewed my decades of knowing, working, and living with her. From this place of emotional upset, I made up stories in my mind, even reinventing a past in which she bossed me around and manipulated situations to her advantage. I was heading for a fight.

Fortunately, this question popped into my mind, "Is there another way to approach this?" I pulled the car off the road and called our mutual friend, coach, and business partner, Marion. "I need help," I started. As usual, she listened with her heart. Because I was asking for help, she gently reminded me of what we were learning from the book *Do You QuantumThink?* Then she asked me a QuantumThink question, "What kind of experience would you like to create?"

As soon as I shifted from my negative, defensive posture to the positive energy of creating, I became clear about what I truly wanted.

"I haven't seen Gail in a year," I replied. "I'd like to have a reunion. I'd like to feel the deep love and support we have for each other." Marion asked, "And would you like to feel heard?" I sat quietly for a moment contemplating this question. "No," I replied. "I don't feel the need to be heard. I do feel the need to hear Gail, though. I realize I have no idea what's going on with her or why she gave me this ultimatum. I'd like to fully hear her."

I thanked Marion and continued on to Gail's home. My experience was completely different than it would have been without pausing for help from my friend. Indeed, as QuantumThink points out, my new intent created an experience that not only changed the present, but the past (my defensive, made-up stories about Gail), and also the future (how our relationship may have been negatively affected if I went in with my boxing gloves on). Gail and I had a loving reunion, and I saw her in all of her magnificence. I asked her, "How are you?" and listened. For forty-five minutes, she talked as we hiked around her beautiful Colorado property. I heard her. We agreed to enter a three-month Quantum-Think program together and address the issue of our partnership again at the end of the program.

The few minutes I spent with our mutual friend and colleague prior to resolving our conflict was priceless. Marion's thoughtful questions led me to envision the best possible experience—and then to live it.

It's only natural to want to be there for our friends and teammates when they are upset. A friend in need is a friend indeed. Occasionally, we will listen without judgment to a friend's relationship issue. The best thing we can then do for them is to gently and firmly redirect them to speak directly with the person with whom they can resolve the issue.

Granted, it might not be a simple problem that can be addressed with a simple conversation (although it may have been simple years ago when it first arose). In its later stages, when a conflict has had time to expand and become deeply entrenched, professional help might be needed—perhaps from a therapist or a mediator. The best advice we can offer our friends and team members is to move their conversation to the people with whom resolution can be found.

Let's not let another day go by without taking this tremendous opportunity to enrich our lives by resolving problems directly and speaking our truth—with compassion. Let's listen without judgment, with our heart. Let's not put another rock into our already heavy emotional backpacks. Instead, let's begin to take those rocks out, one at a time, read the labels on them, and settle unresolved issues that are still festering from past conflicts. Let's lighten our loads and become models for others to do the same. This is Revolutionary Leadership.

# Words of Wisdom

*"I agree to resolve conflicts directly."*

*Out beyond ideas of wrongdoing and rightdoing,*
*there is a field.*
*I'll meet you there.*
—Rumi

*Man must evolve for all human conflict*
*a method which rejects revenge, aggression, and retaliation.*
*The foundation of such a method is love.*
—Martin Luther King, Jr.

*It is one of man's curious idiosyncrasies*
*to create difficulties for the pleasure of resolving them.*
—Joseph de Maistre

*The best way to escape from a problem is to solve it.*
—Alan Saporta

*Peace is not the absence of conflict*
*but the presence of creative alternatives for responding to*
*conflict—alternatives to passive or aggressive responses,*
*alternatives to violence.*
—Dorothy Thompson

*A rumor without a leg to stand on*
*will get around some other way.*
—John Tudor

*The things most people want to know about*
*are usually none of their business.*
—George Bernard Shaw

*Whoever gossips to you*
*will gossip about you.*
—Spanish proverb

*We have war when at least one of the parties to a conflict*
*wants something more than it wants peace.*
—Jeane J. Kirkpatrick

*A good manager doesn't try to eliminate conflict;*
*he tries to keep it from wasting the energies of his people.*
*If you're the boss and your people fight you openly*
*when they think that you are wrong—that's healthy.*
—Robert Townsend

*The greatest conflicts are not between two people*
*but between one person and himself.*
—Garth Brooks

*Peace is not absence of conflict, it is the ability to*
*handle conflict by peaceful means.*
—Ronald Reagan

*When I'm working on a problem, I never think about beauty.*
*I think only how to solve the problem. But when I have finished,*
*if the solution is not beautiful, I know it is wrong.*
—R. Buckminster Fuller

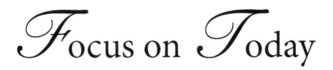

# Focus on Today

*I agree to resolve conflicts directly—TODAY.*

*Here are a few courageous steps you can take to free yourself from unnecessary drama and struggle in your life. Record your thoughts in your journal.*

1. Take the backpack of unresolved conflict rocks off your back today. Then list and label as many rocks as you can: *Example: The day Mom said I looked fat . . . when I heard that my friend L talked badly about me behind my back . . . when my coworker AB didn't do his part of our project and I had to do more work than I should have.*

2. Pick *one* of those labeled rocks to get rid of right now. Begin by writing a letter to the person whose name is on the label, saying everything you want to say to that person—really get everything off your chest. Then destroy the letter with a little ceremony to celebrate lightening your load.

The true test will be the next time you see or even think about that person. Will the strength of that issue have diminished—or even disappeared altogether? If not, *look within* to make sure the issue is indeed with them, and not something unresolved within yourself. If the issue with the other remains strong, seek a way to forgive this person for whatever behavior caused you to carry that rock on your back, remembering, in the words of Malachy McCourt, "Resentment is like taking poison and waiting for the other person to die."

If this works for you, do it with another rock every day until your backpack is empty and you're feeling lighter and freer.

3. Today, as soon as you notice a problem, issue, or complaint you have with someone else, express how you're feeling (speak your truth, with compassion). Speak only for and about yourself and your needs, and refrain from blaming the other. When they reply, listen with your heart.

# $\mathcal{A}$GREEMENT EIGHT

# I agree to honor our choices.

*When we acknowledge that all of life is sacred and that each act is an act of choice and therefore sacred, then life is a sacred dance lived consciously each moment.*
—Scout Cloud Lee

Have you ever beaten yourself up emotionally for a decision you made? Have you ever been harshly critical of others' choices? Does this leave you feeling positive, upbeat, and creative—or negative, distressed, and counterproductive?

*Honor our choices.* If we lived just this one Agreement, our lives would change dramatically. These three words, deeply absorbed into our being, could dispel a lifetime of blame and shame.

*Honor our choices.* Know that we make the best decisions and choices we are capable of in the moment we make them.

## There Are No "Bad" Decisions

Think back to a decision you made in the past, a decision you later regretted. In retrospect, you may very well think of this as a "bad decision." Perhaps you have even felt that it ruined your life. Was it marrying the wrong person and being miserable through all your years together? Taking a job that was so stressful you got sick? Choosing travel over time at home with your children who grew up so suddenly?

Now, consider the moment in which you made your "bad" decision. If you could reconstruct that instant in its every aspect and circumstance, including every thought and experience leading up to it, would you see yourself intentionally choosing something you knew would hurt you? Or would you observe yourself choosing a path that you believed was the best decision for you, based on everything you knew and everything you were feeling at that moment?

Rather than enveloping yourself in blame or regret, acknowledge that this was a choice you made—and *honor your choice.*

Do you recall Agreement Four? "I agree to keep doing what works and change what doesn't." It's also important not to condemn yourself for those things you now decide need changing. You're going to change them. Great. Yet even as you change them, *honor your choices.* Do this and you'll remove yourself from the burdensome path of self judgment. Instead of focusing on what you *should* have done, you'll be taking action (making another choice) to move yourself forward.

Certainly for those of us in second marriages, it can be tempting to call a first marriage a "bad decision." But what good does that do? I could easily wallow in the feeling that I made a poor choice, bemoaning the idea that "I wasted ten years of my life!" and castigating myself for not recognizing and leaving an unhealthy relationship sooner.

Or I can choose to uplift myself by focusing on the positive aspects of my ex-husband and of our relationship, acknowledging the value of what I learned in that relationship that serves me even today.

It's often not easy to have this kind of clarity in the midst of overwhelming emotion, yet it is precisely this ability to disengage from harsh judgment (both of others and of ourselves) that opens up more space for joy in our lives.

For many years following my father's death, I suffered whenever I thought about how I clung to him in his final days. Rather than blessing him, celebrating his life, and letting him know we'd all be okay if it was his time to go, all I seemed to be able to do was literally "hold on for (his) dear life." The fact that he died while I was pleading for him to live haunted me for a long time. Oh, if only I had been able to offer him sweetness and love in his final hours, rather than projecting my fears of his approaching death onto him, along with bitterness towards the doctors whom I blamed.

Looking back years later, I realized that losing Dad had been a new experience for me. I had never lost a parent before and wasn't prepared—and I did the best I knew how under the circumstances. I was on a mission to save his life, and I had a learning experience. Once I could see this, I could make new and different decisions about how I would relate to my mother's final years.

I was never able to speak with my father about the inevitability of his death. Today I can speak openly and lovingly with my mother about hers.

"Mom, do you ever think about the fact that you are closer to the end of your life than to the beginning?" I asked one day. She replied, "No . . . and you wouldn't think so either if you saw how I shopped. I'm buying things that will last me another fifty years!"

I no longer take my mother for granted as if she will go on living forever. I take care to express my love frequently and I will continue doing so until the day that she passes. This is something I learned from the different choices I made—and that I now honor—regarding my father.

Perhaps the greatest choice we have is how we feel about our present circumstances. And this includes how we feel about the myriad of decisions that have led to now. Rather than judging ourselves based on the outcome of each decision, what if we loved ourselves (and others) for the courage to make the choices we make every day?

We do the best we can. You. Your spouse. Your boss. Your parents, children, neighbors . . . everyone with whom you come into contact. We all make the best choices or decisions we are capable of in that moment.

## There Are No "Mistakes"

I used to be very hard on myself. My longtime need for others to like me and think I excelled at whatever I was doing created a tremendous amount of stress in my life.

One day my favorite boss and mentor, Mary Ruth, called me into her office and asked, "Marian, do you expect your husband to be perfect?" Puzzled as to why she might be asking this question, I replied honestly, "No, of course not."

Then she asked, "Do you expect the managers who report to you to be perfect?" Ahh . . . now I thought I understood. Someone must have made a big mistake, and this was her way of gently letting me know about it. I answered truthfully, "No, of course not."

Then came her punch line: "Then why do you think *you* have to be perfect?"

I learned from the ensuing conversation that my pattern of self-criticism was not only unhealthy for me, it also created stress and unnecessary drama for others in my workplace.

Now, many years later, that stressed-out sense of always needing to feel perfect is gone. In its place is the contentment of knowing and living this Revolutionary Agreement to the best of my ability. When I embody this Agreement, I spend less time beating myself up and more time learning from my decisions. I spend less time blaming myself and others and more time accepting and moving on.

James Burke tells a wonderful story of his early days at Johnson & Johnson. After Burke's first major project as head of a new products division had failed, CEO Robert Wood Johnson called him into his office and asked if Burke was the one who had just cost them all that money.

"I thought I was going to get fired," he recalled in *Fortune* (December 26, 1994). Instead, Johnson said, "I want to congratulate you. Business is about taking risks. Keep doing it." [1]

At the Neenan Company in Fort Collins, Colorado, a gong reverberates through the halls of the workplace when someone notices a mistake. When the gong sounds, the staff eagerly ask one another, "What was the mistake?" so they can learn from it. It's their culture to celebrate what they call "learning experiences" rather than punishing what other companies would call "mistakes."

Thinking of myself as a "learner" and using the term "learning experience" in place of the word "mistake" has helped me to embody this Agreement. It may do the same for you.

*I recently told my daughter that I was not happy about my behavior at a meeting I attended. I felt I was reactive and not my best self. "It's ok to make a mistake, Mom," she said gently.*

*For some reason it hit me between the eyes. "Wow. Of course. I made a mistake. I could apologize if need be, learn something from it, and move on."*

*It's amazing how tough we can be on ourselves, isn't it? And we can also be tough on each other. This Agreement*

151

*is a way to remember, "We are each doing the best we can in that moment." We can learn to make another decision and move on.*

*After the meeting, I knew I hadn't been my best self. But I also knew that I hadn't been intentionally trying to be less than my best. That's how it is. It's called the spirituality of imperfection. We are human beings each making the best decisions we can in the moment. Otherwise we'd be making different ones! [2]*

*—Martie*

## In Perspective

Some days I'm better at practicing this Agreement than others.

I've found myself in situations where I would be tempted to say, "There goes Glenn, off to lunch again with his buddies—eating unhealthy food and spending money unnecessarily when there's food in our refrigerator." Yet when I notice my judgment arise, I'd think of this Agreement, consciously shift my attitude and instead say to myself, "Isn't it great that Glenn has such good friends and that they so enjoy having lunch together?"

I was judgmental about one of my capable colleagues when she decided not to put in the extra effort to earn an incentive cruise. When I noticed that I was thinking she was "lazy," I remembered this Agreement and forced myself to think of some other possibilities. She may have had other plans already on the dates of the cruise, so it wouldn't be worth the effort to earn it. Maybe she (or her husband) gets seasick, so the cruise wasn't appealing. Or perhaps the company's incentive may not have been hers—she may have been more interested in spending time with her family or other personal pursuits. I really didn't know.

And that's exactly the point. Most of the time, we *don't* know and *can't* know why people make the choices they do. We simply don't have the whole perspective.

Many years ago, a wise speaker made a life-changing impact on me when he said, "Unless you know a person's complete history, all that he has experienced in the past and all that is intended for his future, there is no way you can judge him for what he does today."

Even with the best of intentions regarding desired outcomes, our decisions are not isolated events. Every choice connects with others' choices to render an outcome that is beyond our knowing. As Stephen Covey writes, "While we are free to choose our actions, we are not free to choose the consequences of those actions." [3]

I would add that we are free to choose our *attitude* towards those consequences. To take it a step further, QuantumThinking taught me to consciously create a context for my experience of life—independent of circumstances. If the framework I choose to adopt is that everything happens in perfection—even if it is beyond my mind's comprehension to see how in the moment—then I can relax and let go of the self-imposed burden of judging. This applies equally to judging circumstances as it does to human behavior.

> *Unless we are looking from the whole, seeing life from the largest perspective that we are calling the Perspective of All Perspectives, we can very possibly miss something that may be related to a result we are after but don't immediately see the relationship of. This is why we suggest that to achieve a state of mastery requires developing the Perspective of all Perspectives. This is the ability to be open to the idea that* anything *that shows up is valuable even when we disagree with it, because it's likely to be a contributing factor in the*

*result we want to produce, particularly when the result we are after is unprecedented.*

*Suppose you are in charge of creating a new marketing campaign for your company's product. You and your team come up with what you deem to be the perfect slogan. Everyone is jazzed. The next day you are reading the industry news and find out your competitor has already come out with the nearly identical slogan. Will you and your team's passion be dampened? Not when you maintain the Perspective of all Perspectives. Momentarily unnerved you speedily regain your equanimity. You call your team and decide to regroup at the nearby coffee shop. You're sitting there and you casually glance at the woman at the next table reading a book with the exact word in the title that jumps out at everyone as the key to a much spicier slogan for the product.*

*From the old worldview of separation, we tend to see an unexpected event as an interruption or an obstacle along our path. From a new worldview of wholeness, we look deeper to see the wisdom in this seeming obstacle showing up, knowing it is part of the whole picture and realizing there is value to be gleaned from it."*

*—from* Do You QuantumThink?[4]

## Acceptance and Forgiveness

At the core of this Agreement, at its very deepest meaning, a question arises concerning forgiveness. It is, "If I truly accept our choices with no judgment, then is there any need for forgiveness?"

Forgiveness has its rightful place. For example, when someone forgives their childhood abuser or the murderer of a loved one, it may release them from living the rest of their life with debilitating emotions like anger and resentment. True forgiveness can free them to be the fullest expression of their divine Self. The "philosopher of happiness," Jonathan Lockwood Huie, offers his perspective, "Forgive others, not because they deserve forgiveness, but because you deserve peace."

Nelson Mandela was perhaps the greatest living example of someone who—despite twenty-seven years of incarceration and countless atrocities to the people he loved—exemplified love and forgiveness. In one of his many courageous acts, he invited the state prosecutor to dinner thirty-two years after the prosecutor had convicted Mandela of sabotage and demanded the death penalty. Mandela said of this man that he had only been doing his job. Might we say that he honored the prosecutor's choice to do his job well?

As a volunteer for our community's restorative justice program, aptly named Teaching Peace, I have participated in an innovative approach to dealing with criminal offenders in our society. Founded on principles and practices of indigenous peoples—such as ho'oponopono, the ancient Hawaiian cultural practice of reconciliation and forgiveness—restorative justice offers the victim an opportunity to be heard and the offender an opportunity to repair the harms he or she caused by their actions.

In our program, the offender and victim, each with a close friend or family member, sit in a circle with community members and the arresting officer. Two trained facilitators invite each person in turn to speak about the incident in order to identify all the harms. Everyone there then works together to create a contract that the offender must keep to stay out of the punitive system involving court and jail. The contract focuses on repairing as many of the harms created by the offender's actions as possible. By getting the fullest possible picture of the consequences of their choices, offenders are more likely to make different choices in the future. Indeed, statistics show that this community restorative justice program results in only a ten percent rearrest rate, whereas the national recidivism average for those who go through our punitive justice system has been as high as seventy percent.

Restorative justice offers an opportunity to practice most of the Revolutionary Agreements, from *listen with your heart, speak your truth with compassion,* and *change what doesn't work,* to *respect our differences, see the best in others,* and of course *resolve conflicts directly.* That was one of the many reasons why serving our community's restorative justice program was so fulfilling for me.

In the words of ho'oponopono teacher Kahuna Morrnah Nalamaku Simeona, "If we can accept that we are the sum total of all past thoughts, emotions, words, deeds, and actions and that our present lives and choices are colored or shaded by this memory bank of the past, then we begin to see how a process of correcting or setting aright can change our lives, our families, and our society." [5]

I am not suggesting we accept violent behavior. I am asking that we notice our judgment about the choices we all make every day. What would it be like if instead of being quick to criticize, we practiced acceptance more? Now that's revolutionary! I find that the more I practice acceptance, the less I need to practice forgiveness.

As we release our judgments and accept that we make the best possible choices we are capable of in the moment, we contribute to a revolution of genuinely epic proportion. Honoring our choices engenders greater peace in our minds and hearts, which in turn, contributes to Peace on Earth.

# Words of Wisdom

*"I agree to honor our choices."*

*Hindsight is always twenty-twenty.*
—Billy Wilder

*There are no mistakes; none have ever been made*
*and none ever will be made.*
—Ernest Holmes

*Whatever humans have learned had to be learned*
*as a consequence only of trial and error experience.*
*Humans have learned only through mistakes.*
—R. Buckminster Fuller

*Great Spirit, help me never to judge another until I have walked*
*in his moccasins.*
—Sioux Indian prayer

*In any moment of decision, the best thing you can do is the*
*right thing, the next best thing is the wrong thing, and the*
*worst thing you can do is nothing.*
—Theodore Roosevelt

*Nothing is more difficult, and therefore more precious,*
*than to be able to decide.*
—Napoleon Bonaparte

*There is simply no such thing as a correct decision.*
*Life is far too complicated for that.*
—Tom Peters

*If a woman has to choose between catching a fly ball and saving*
*an infant's life, she will choose to save the infant's life without*
*even considering if there are men on base.*
—Dave Barry

*If you have made mistakes, even serious ones,*
*there is always another chance for you. You may have a fresh*
*start any moment you choose, for this thing we call failure*
*is not the falling down but the staying down.*
—Mary Pickford

*The nice thing about standards is that there are so many*
*of them to choose from.*
—Andrew S. Tanenbaum

*No man chooses evil because it is evil; he only mistakes it for*
*happiness, the good he seeks.*
—Mary Wollstonecraft

*All our final decisions are made in a state of mind that*
*is not going to last.*
—Marcel Proust

*Choose your love; Love your choice.*
—Thomas S. Monson

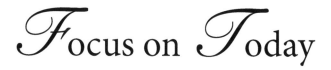

# Focus on Today

*I agree to honor our choices—TODAY.*

*Here are a few steps that will start you down the path of being less judgmental and more accepting, leading you to experience unconditional love. Record your thoughts in your journal.*

1. Explore the reasons you made what you now consider "bad decisions." What were you thinking/feeling at the time of each decision?

   *Decision: I followed the doctor's advice and gave my son massive amounts of antibiotics to attempt to kill the Lyme bacteria.*

   *Reason: I wanted to do everything possible to cure Michael of this debilitating disease as quickly as possible. I was frightened. I knew that the longer it stayed in his body the more havoc it would wreak.*

   *Outcome: It is unlikely the antibiotics had any effect, except possibly to weaken Michael's immune system. An unconventional method we used was what ultimately worked. At the time of the decision to use antibiotics, I made the best choice I knew how.*

2. Celebrate every "mistake" you make today, consciously reframing each one as a fortunate learning experience.

   *What happened: I searched everywhere for the phone I had misplaced. The ringer was turned off so calling it was fruitless.*

   *Learning: This is not the first time I have done this. It's time for me to choose a specific place in each part of my home where I put my phone so I don't have to experience the frustration of searching for it when I need it.*

3. Take the time to consider whether you're being unnecessarily judgmental about others' choices.
   *Example: I am critical about someone I work with who I believe would be more fit if he exercised some of the time, rather than spending his days sitting at his computer and in meetings.*

Then ask yourself: "Does it serve either of us to carry around this judgment? Do I know this person's complete history, including all the experiences that brought this person to this point?"

   *Example: Maybe he has weak knees or hips or heart or for some other medical reason cannot comfortably exercise. Some people don't have enough "get up and go" to actually get up and go!*

# $\mathcal{G}$RATITUDE

*To speak gratitude is courteous and pleasant,
to enact gratitude is generous and noble,
but to live gratitude is to touch Heaven.*
—Johannes A. Gaertner

# $\mathcal{G}$RATITUDE

*I AGREE TO:*

*Give and receive thanks.*
*See the best in myself and others.*
*Look for blessings in disguise.*
*Lighten up!*

The word *gratitude* shares the same root as the words "grace" and "gracious." To be "grateful" means to be full of pleasure and steeped in grace; to be awash in a sense of delight at all the wonders, the blessings, the deliriously, deliciously exquisite joys of life unfolding on all sides.

The last set of Agreements are all aspects of this state of grace.

Gratitude has to do with developing the habit of seeing what's right rather than what's wrong; of seeing the best in everything around us.

Does this mean blinding ourselves to "the realities" of life? On the contrary, it means shining our light onto the darkness as we embrace it. It is no coincidence that the last Agreement is to "lighten up." All four Agreements in this third group have to do with creating a life filled with love, light, and delight.

*Love is the light of life,*
*Happiness is the delight of life.*
—Debasish Mridha

# $\mathcal{A}$GREEMENT NINE

# I agree to give
# and receive thanks.

*There is more hunger for love and appreciation*
*in this world than for bread.*
—Mother Teresa[1]

Voicing appreciation for others is helpful. Letting people know when you see them doing their best encourages them to keep going for it. But being *truly grateful* for another's actions and contributions . . . now that's life-changing.

## Gift of Gratitude

As our twenty-fourth wedding anniversary approached, I became acutely aware of how critical I had been of Glenn during the previous year. Although my criticism had to do with one of our businesses, my frustration and anger had spilled over into other aspects of our relationship. For nearly a year I was on edge, and I wanted to push him over it! As angry as I felt, I did not want to cause my marriage to end. What to do?

Practicing the old adage, "We teach what we need to learn," I recalled my own words:

*Gratitude has to do with developing the habit of seeing what's right rather than what's wrong; of seeing the best in everything around us.*

Somehow I had gotten into the habit of focusing on the opposite. If Glenn and I were going to be together to celebrate our twenty-fifth wedding anniversary, I knew I was going to have to change my attitude. I decided to cultivate an "attitude of gratitude" and committed to writing down one thing I appreciated about him every day. Every morning I focused on what I liked about him in that moment. I built a new "habit of seeing what's right." Without asking Glenn to do anything differently, my anger lifted and I found myself falling in love with him again.

*The power of gratitude is like an ocean wave. With beauty and subtlety, it can lighten and move the heaviest load.*

Glenn didn't know I was writing a gratitude journal dedicated solely to him. It became the perfect gift to surprise him with for our twenty-fifth wedding anniversary. Now six years later, our life together is magnificent. Last year Glenn suggested I publish a book about the journal in the hope it may help others struggling with their relationships. Although it is quite intimate, I agreed to produce *Gratitude Journal for a Healthy Marriage*.[2] May it bless others as it continues to bless us.

## Gratitude For Things To Come

Experiencing the fullness of gratitude for what is in front of us is a wonderful feeling, yet there is a deeper level of gratitude—giving thanks for what *we don't yet have.*

Can you imagine how much better we'd all feel if instead of worrying about something, we celebrated and felt gratitude for the outcomes we desire and can picture in our minds? In fact, being grateful for something we envision makes it more likely we will actually experience it—that it *will* happen. Great athletes and successful professionals know how to visualize the future and pour their emotions into the imagined outcome as though it was currently happening.

Using our program, "VisionWorks: Setting Your Sights on Success!" Glenn and I used to guide teams through envisioning their ideal work situation from an imaginary future vantage point, looking back in time to celebrate extraordinary accomplishments. With an uplifting feeling of gratitude for having reached the pinnacle of success, each team member imagined the workplace in its highest possible state, from the physical environment to the way in which they communicated with one another. They then shared their visions with each other. Everything was captured on flip charts around the room, priorities were set, and teams self-selected to set and implement the strategies to create their combined vision.

This groundbreaking process (which Glenn initiated in the 1970s) produced results that would not have been possible without the ability to feel gratitude for something that hadn't yet happened—to become, as Norman Vincent Peale termed it, "possibilitarians."

The act of envisioning and feeling gratitude is sometimes enough in itself to create far-reaching changes, even without additional action. Significantly, studies point to a link between gratitude and good health.[3]

One of my mentors, best friends, and business partners, Marion Culhane, taught me through practical application that *what we focus our attention and intention on is what we get*. If we focus on lack, then lack is what we'll have. If we focus on anticipated failures, then failures will more likely befall us. And if we focus on gratitude, then we experience even more to be grateful for.

## Daily Gratitude

One of my most cherished memories is of our young son, Michael's, bedtime routine. Glenn and I would sit at the edge of his bed and together light a candle in his darkened room. The bright flame signified the light of God. Each of us in turn would express our gratitude for everything we could think of. It was so much fun to hear what Michael came up with each day! Then we would blow out the candle together, knowing that God's light is always in each of us.

> *Expressing gratitude is a daily ritual (truly a daily delight!) for my family and me. We began a nightly tradition when my youngest was a toddler, completing each dinner by going around the table with each person sharing what they are grateful for or happy about from that day. It's illuminating to pause and reflect on what brings us joy. Not only has this expanded our awareness and appreciation of every-day blessings, it's also deepened our understanding of and connection to one another. It's a gift in itself to listen to and celebrate my sons' joyful moments from the day.*
>
> *My personal gratitude journal also has served me in cultivating and expanding my joy and appreciation. I have kept one for years. Some people choose to write down a set number of things (at least one, or perhaps three, four, or five) they are grateful for each day. I tend to approach my expression of gratitude as a stream of consciousness, and the number of items I write down varies. I keep my gratitude journal by my bed. Writing in it is the last thing I do before I turn off the light each night.*
> —*Stacey*

From morning until night, from the people in our lives to the Source of our lives, we have an abundance of opportunities to feel and express appreciation. It is magical to fill our lives with countless moments of gratitude both by *noticing* them more and by *creating* more of them. Yet in our busy lives, it can seem as if days (and weeks and months) go by in a flash, without us giving thought or voice to what we appreciate. Might there be a specific time every day that you would like to focus on what you are grateful for? I do so every morning during my morning walk or bike ride in Nature. I look forward to this precious time every day.

## True Wealth

During the Global Forum of Spiritual and Parliamentary Leaders on Human Survival in Oxford, I overheard a conversation with Mother Teresa that affected me deeply. Responding to a despairing comment about the poor people she served, she said something like, "Some people I have worked with in impoverished environments are not as poor as some of the wealthiest people of the West. Their richness is of the heart and the Spirit; their love of God gives them peace of mind."

This richness she spoke of is accessible to each of us, right in this moment, and in every moment. The doorway to achieving it is the feeling and expression of gratitude. One of the most profoundly happy times in my life involved sending an annual letter to about one hundred fifty people I care about. Although the content of the letter was the same for each person, I took the time to consider what it was about each person that I was grateful for. On the bottom of each person's preprinted letter, I wrote a personal note thanking them for the special way they blessed my life. It took about two weeks for me to finish my personal notes. That day I said to Glenn, "If my life were to end today, I would die happily. I feel completely fulfilled."

It is such a joy to sincerely thank people for what they offer to life. Yet many people devote more energy to bringing other people down than to building them up. From the time we are teased (or tease others) on the playground to the day we join in gossip around the proverbial water cooler at work, we are immersed in a culture that fosters negativity. With these societal norms, it can take character and emotional fortitude to express appreciation for others. The rewards are well worth the effort.

Classical singer Marian Anderson achieved great success despite unspeakable racial discrimination throughout her life. I took to heart these words of hers, "As long as you keep a person down, some part of you has to be down there to hold him down, so it means you cannot soar as you might otherwise."[4]

Imagine a room full of people putting down others and another room next door filled with people expressing their appreciation for others. Where would you rather be?

## Receiving Thanks

Receiving thanks is as important as giving thanks, for one cannot exist fully without the other. Yet while most of us are taught how to say "Thank you," it is a rare thing indeed for people to be taught how to receive thanks.

Can you remember the last time you thanked someone, only to have that person respond by looking away and changing the subject, or making a joke, or saying, "Oh, it was nothing." Do you remember how this felt? By minimizing or deflecting your appreciation, they short-circuited it. In a very real sense, they *denied* it. Most likely they did so without any intention of dishonoring your thanks; it's just how many of us have been raised. But intentionally or not, in that moment your expression of thanks was dishonored.

> *I had a friend who was a gifted musician. After his concerts, I would tell him how wonderful I thought his perform-ance was. He would inevitably dismiss what I said with something like, "Oh, the tenors were flatter than road*

*kill," or "In that run in the second movement, the sopranos sounded like they were falling down a flight of stairs." On and on he would go, pointing out all the flaws in the performance. It made me feel horrible, as if there was something wrong with me that I loved and appreciated the concert.*

*I remember consciously deciding not to do that to others. If someone thanked me, I would practice saying, "You're welcome," plain and simple. Nothing more was needed— no defense, no deflection, no making a joke, no pointing out my mistakes or imperfections. I came to see that just those little words, "You're welcome," were a way to receive the gift of gratitude and honor the other person. The irony is that the more we deflect a thank you, the more we are actually making it about us, when in fact saying and receiving thanks is not about us at all! It is about living in the Divine flow of the energy of grace.[5]*

*—Martie*

This Agreement asks us to accept acknowledgment graciously and fully. Receiving thanks means *letting it in.* In Western culture, it means looking into the eyes of the one appreciating us, uncrossing our arms, smiling and breathing in the acknowledgment. "You're welcome," may be appropriate, or "It was my pleasure," if that's the truth. Or perhaps, "Thank you for your acknowledgment," spoken from your heart. The exact words matter less; the spirit of it means everything. In so doing, the cycle of gratitude is fulfilled.

## Thanking Ourselves

As little as we tend to be taught about receiving thanks, we tend to be taught even less about appreciating and thanking *ourselves* for the contributions we make.

When Michael was a child, I read the book, *Punished by Rewards: The Trouble with Gold Stars, Incentive Plans, A's, Praise, and Other Bribes.*[6] It had a profound effect on me. Rightly or wrongly, I held back from praising Michael for many years and instead encouraged him to acknowledge himself. "How did that make you feel?" I might ask, instead of saying, "That was great! I'm so proud of you." Whether my words contributed to his self-reliant character—or impaired him or our relationship in any way—I don't know for sure. Looking back, I think a combination of directing him to his own internal meter *and* expressing my awe at his accomplishments might have been optimal.

As adults, we are taught that our employer or supervisor is responsible for acknowledging our work. Can you imagine a boss who would say, "Be sure to let me know when you feel you've done something worthy of my notice."? Yet that's just what Glenn and I have done.

When hiring staff for one of our consulting jobs, we asked a young applicant if he could accept our Team Agreements. At the time, this particular Agreement read, "I agree to take responsibility for acknowledging myself." He was adamant that this was not his responsibility, "As your employee, I think it's *your* job to acknowledge me."

I told him, "We're usually on top of noticing and acknowledging our team members' contributions—but what if we miss something? What if you were to make a contribution that saved our client thousands of dollars . . . and no one noticed? How would you feel? Why feel unappreciated for even one moment? Why not celebrate your successes by claiming your contribution with joy, 'Guess what I've done,' or even, 'Hey! I deserve a medal for this one!'"

We sometimes go about life feeling unappreciated for our contributions, yet without the know-how or permission to articulate our successes. Glenn and I created a way to raise self-appreciation at one of our client's sites. We encouraged them to institute "bragging rights" as part of their regular staff meetings. What a great way to find out what's working in your organization—and to allow people to share the joys of their accomplishments. With practice, this Agreement can become easy and fun.

When we appreciate something, *it appreciates in value*. Imagine all of the aspects of our lives—relationships, finances, work, health, and more—increasing in value as we speak and receive more words of gratitude. The world will be forever grateful.

# Words of Wisdom

*"I agree to give and receive thanks."*

*I would maintain that thanks are the highest form of thought,
and that gratitude is happiness doubled by wonder.*
—Gilbert K. Chesterton

*Gratitude unlocks the fullness of life. It turns what we have into
enough, and more. It turns denial into acceptance, chaos to
order, confusion to clarity. It can turn a meal into a feast,
a house into a home, a stranger into a friend. Gratitude
makes sense of our past, brings peace for today,
and creates a vision for tomorrow.*
—Melody Beattie

*I've learned that people will forget what you said, people
will forget what you did, but people will never forget
how you made them feel.*
—Maya Angelou

*Let us be grateful to people who make us happy; they are the
charming gardeners who make our souls blossom.*
—Marcel Proust

*Feeling gratitude and not expressing it is like wrapping
a present and not giving it.*
—William Arthur Ward

*Make it a habit to tell people thank you. To express your appreciation, sincerely and without the expectation of anything in return. Truly appreciate those around you, and you'll soon find many others around you. Truly appreciate life, and you'll find that you have more of it.*
—Ralph Marston

*You have it easily in your power to increase the sum total of this world's happiness now. How? By giving a few words of sincere appreciation to someone who is lonely or discouraged. Perhaps you will forget tomorrow the kind words you say today, but the recipient may cherish them over a lifetime.*
—Dale Carnegie

*Gratitude is something of which none of us can give too much. For on the smiles, the thanks we give, our little gestures of appreciation, our neighbors build their philosophy of life.*
—A.J. Cronin

*Appreciative words are the most powerful force for good on earth!*
—George W. Crane

*Gratitude is the fairest blossom which springs from the soul.*
—Henry Ward Beecher

*One is taught by experience to put a premium on those few people who can appreciate you for what you are.*
—Gail Godwin

*If the only prayer you ever say in your entire life is "Thank you," it will be enough.*
—Meister Eckhart

# Focus on Today

*I agree to give and receive thanks—TODAY.*

*Here are several steps you can take to enjoy saying "thank you" more often and receiving appreciation from others more fully. Doing so, you can expect to have a better than average day. Record your thoughts in your journal.*

1.  What are you grateful for in this very moment?
    *Example: My wise and fun new girlfriends here in Kauai. The opportunity to share Tai Ji Dance with my friend and student today. Meeting participants in a Revolutionary Agreements program in California via Skype an hour ago. The exquisite beauty of my surroundings. Practicing uplifting songs today for our Sacred Earth Choir concert. (All that gratitude bubbled up in only seconds!)*

2.  Pick three of the items above and express your thanks directly to those involved, within the next twenty-four hours. Notice the experience of expressing your thanks to these three people and their responses. Record this in your journal.

3.  Every time someone thanks you for something today, uncross your arms and look them in the eyes (if culturally appropriate), smile, take a deep breath and say, "You're welcome," or, "My pleasure," and nothing else. Record in your journal how this felt.
    *Example: A friend thanked me for singing a special song for her. I felt embarrassed and said, "It's not really my key." She asked me to simply say, "Thank you," and receive her praise. (Ha!) I started again, looked at her, smiled, and said, "Thank you." I felt appreciative and appreciated.*

# $\mathcal{A}$GREEMENT TEN

# I agree to see the best in myself and others.

*The potential of the average person is like a huge ocean unsailed, a new continent unexplored, a world of possibilities waiting to be released and channeled toward some great good.*
—Brian Tracy

C ome with me for a moment on a journey back to your childhood. Imagine yourself sitting at your desk in your elementary school classroom.

*The teacher asks a question. The child next to you shoots her hand into the air and is called upon. She answers the question thoughtfully and beautifully, and after she's finished the entire class cheers at the top of their lungs. Everyone can tell what a wonderful answer it was.*

*The teacher smiles broadly and allows the hubbub to continue until it dies down naturally. All are eager for the next lesson. The teacher captivates everyone as she brings history to life in her dramatic retelling. She asks how this story applies to something that's happened to you recently . . . and waits to see who will volunteer an answer.*

*Now it's your hand that shoots up into the air with confidence, and she calls on you expectantly. You share your thoughts on how the story shows that history repeats itself, and the class again explodes into applause, thrilled at the insight and power of your thoughts.*

*In the hallway after class, one of your classmates pats you on the back and compliments you on your creative answer. Once again, you've been validated.*

*You are, in fact, being groomed for a lifetime of giving your best. Seeing the best in others comes naturally to you, as does supporting others to do the same. It has been taught, encouraged, and rewarded for so long, it has simply become a way of life.*

Okay, perhaps this is not how your normal school day was. But what if it had been, day after day, year after year? How would that have affected you? What abilities, skills, and pathways in life would this kind of extraordinarily nurturing, supportive environment have opened up for you?

Here is the wonderful thing: *It's not too late.* We can create a nurturing environment, today and every day. That's what this Agreement is all about.

In our family, we used to create a weekly theme in the form of a question to ponder each night at the dinner table. During "kindness week," we would ask (and answer), "Who was kind to me today?" and "Who was I kind to?" During "encouragement" week," we would ask, "Who encouraged me today—and whom did I encourage?" These questions gave us an opportunity to see the best in others and ourselves.

Barbara Marx Hubbard saw the best in me and helped me on the path to overcoming my tendency to be motivated by others' approval. While working on a project together, Barbara said, "Marian, the only thing holding you back from making the greatest possible contribution to the world is your need for approval. When you're able to release that, you'll be able to achieve your heart's desire and be an unstoppable force for good in the world."

Barbara's seeing the best in me is what gave me the courage to take steps to let go of my long-held need for approval, and this did indeed open the door to a more creative, positive life.

## Nurture Your Best

To see the best in myself and others is to see ourselves created in God's image. As we enter this life, we are each endowed with innate wisdom, then given life experiences to learn to be our truest Self. We are challenged to stretch to new limits, break through them to experience new horizons, and support one another in achieving ever higher levels of mastery.

My son, Michael, sees the best in everyone. Having been a competitive gymnast and now a coach, his philosophy is, "Anybody can do anything they want, as long as they take small steps and practice." He certainly didn't start out being able to do the iron cross on the rings, but after many small steps and much practice he was able to achieve the state title for first place in rings. We all have everything we need to be our best. When we recognize this in others—as Michael does with those he coaches—it can have a profound effect on both parties.

Imagine being surrounded by people who always see the best in you. The art of love is bringing out the best in others while being your best self.

*One of my business clients was concerned about losing productivity at work. At a closer look, we discovered that the root of the problem was at home. His insistence that his wife support him by acting in ways he deemed "right" was draining his energy.*

177

> *I suggested that he use the Agreement "to see the best in myself and others" and requested, "Why don't you talk with your wife about only what she's doing right for the next week?" He did so, and the result was nothing less than transformative. Both his relationship with his wife and his productivity at work experienced a dramatic turnaround.*
> —Laurie

## The Revolutionary Leader

Living this Agreement is the essence of what it means to be a Revolutionary Leader: *One who fosters an environment of genuine collaboration among people who see the best in each other.*

In the 1970s, we often heard the phrase "leaderless" groups. This concept was borne of the effort to shed the shackles of authoritarian leadership and promote creativity and synergy.

But seeing the best in each other does not foster leaderless groups. On the contrary, it promotes leader*ful* groups—organizations, communities, and households wherein every participant is encouraged to take the lead when he or she knows what to do next. The eyes take over when it's time to see and the ears tune in when it's time to hear. Each member has his or her function and naturally expresses their individual potential for the benefit of all. The group thus led is an organic entity—the organization as living organism.

Being a Revolutionary Leader requires the skills of a mediator and facilitator, not a courtroom lawyer or authoritarian. A Revolutionary Leader is one who fosters an environment of genuine collaboration toward agreed-upon actions that serve the greatest whole. This requires patience, compassion, humility, and love. The result is the magic of synergy, where the power of one plus one is far greater than two.

*As part of the Soviet Center for International Dialogue (created by my wife Rama in the mid 1980s), we were called upon to facilitate communication for the positive growth and reintegration of transitional and sometimes adversarial communities. One such assignment called us to go abroad and work with delegations from Armenia and Azerbaijan. There was so much anger and pain that neither side was willing to meet and negotiations were at a standstill.*

*We began working with each group separately in their own territories, listening deeply with our hearts, and gently facilitating the full expression of each person's story and feelings about the Armenian and Azerbaijani conflict. Eventually, the two groups agreed to meet in the neutral territory of Georgia. In a large room we gathered around a table, the Armenians grouped on one side and the Azerbaijanis on the other. The air crackled with tension. Rama and I held this precious and fragile space as one of safety and possibility.*

*Eventually, an Azerbaijani man took the initiative and passionately poured his heart out. He spoke of walking hand-in-hand with his young son when accosted by a Red Army soldier who demanded to see his papers. Throwing his papers into the blood and gore on the street, the soldier forced the Azerbaijani to crawl on his hands and knees to retrieve them with his teeth. As he told us his story, he cried, lamenting that his son would always see him as weak because of losing face in that most humiliating moment.*

*The depth of this man's pain permeated the silence in our room. Suddenly, an Armenian man from across the huge table got up from his chair, stretched his body across the table and reached out with his hand, fingers pointed toward the Azerbaijani. Choked with emotion, he said, "You sound just like me."*

*In that moment the energy of the room shifted and people began, one-by-one, to share their personal stories, discovering that they had similar feelings, hopes, and a deep desire for peace. As each participant felt truly heard, healing began and they could listen to each other more deeply. Ultimately, they began to see the best in themselves and each other (one of my favorite Revolutionary Agreements).*

*That night and for the next two days, former enemies who had never talked or touched each other became fast friends, shared meals together, and made commitments to continue dialogue and work together on joint peace projects.*
*—Max*

Revolutionary Leadership creates a new dynamic—the leader who doesn't have to know everything nor pretend to. David Neenan shares a story about a pivotal event in the evolution of his multi-million dollar Neenan Company during a particularly challenging time in the company's history. At a board meeting with the heads of his departments, realizing that he simply didn't know what to do to turn their dire circumstances around, he looked around the room and said with utter candor, "I don't have the slightest idea what to do here." No one spoke. Then one brave soul said, "Well . . . why don't we work together? We've tried everything else."

Some might have called David's admission a lack of leadership. I call it Revolutionary Leadership. David says the company's future owed a great deal to this shift to collaborative leadership.

This is a vastly different scenario from a dog-eat-dog environment, with everyone doing his level best to scramble up the ladder to success while heedlessly stepping on anyone and everyone along the way. To be great, one does not need to be *better than*. The joy of being a Revolutionary Leader is exhilarating.

What would it look like to see the best in everyone in your own workplace? To foster an environment of genuine appreciation and collaboration? What simple steps can you take to help create or further develop an environment in which your teammates feel empowered to express their individual and collective potential?

> *Recurring communication issues with a colleague developed into a contentious relationship and began impacting our entire work environment. I took out the Agreements and assessed the situation and my reaction to it. Did I want my relationship with this person to be one of conflict or one of acceptance, gratitude, and compassion? I realized that I wanted this situation to be different. I also realized that I had a choice and that I could make the decision to live by the Agreements in my business life.*
>
> *The next time I met with my colleague I chose to see her as someone with skill, competence, and spirit; and as a partner, not an adversary. The commitment to see only the best in her transformed my body language, choice of words, tone of voice, and energy. The result was an incredible feeling of mutual understanding and respect and the conflict simply fell away.*
> —Lisa

This model of Revolutionary Leadership is not for the workplace alone. It is equally practical—and equally powerful—in the home. Think of your home for a moment. Is there one household member who lords it over the rest? What might it be like if all members of your household were allowed, even encouraged, to express themselves fully, and take the lead naturally, creating a dance of leading, following, collaborating . . . leading, following, collaborating?

*I see the best in you.* I know that you can be a Revolutionary Leader of the highest order. That you can excel in all that you do, with the grace that follows commitment and the joy that emanates from contribution.

*I see the best in you.* I see you enjoying the journey along the path of excellence, creativity, and fulfillment.

*I see the best in you.* I hold you as fully capable of creating your own reality and making choices that foster peace in your life and cocreate Peace on Earth.

*I see the best in you.*

# Words of Wisdom

*"I agree to see the best in myself and others."*

*Hide not your talents. They for use were made.*
*What's a sundial in the shade?*
—Benjamin Franklin

*For some strange reason I can never be what I ought to be until*
*you are what you ought to be. And you can never be what you*
*ought to be until I am what I ought to be. This is the way*
*God's universe is made; this is the way it is structured.*
—Dr. Martin Luther King, Jr.

*When do you become the person you want to quote? Your time is*
*now. Awaken to your own greatness, to your own magnificence.*
*You are the icon of your own life.*
—Dianne Collins

*Everyone has inside of him a piece of good news. The good news*
*is that you don't know how great you can be! How much you can*
*love! What you can accomplish! And what your potential is!*
—Anne Frank

*I know of no more encouraging fact than the unquestionable*
*ability of man to elevate his life by conscious endeavor.*
—Henry David Thoreau

*One of the sanest, surest, and most generous joys of life comes from being happy over the good fortune of others.*
—Archibald Rutledge

*If human beings are perceived as potentials rather than problems, as possessing strengths instead of weaknesses, as unlimited rather than dull and unresponsive, then they thrive and grow to their capabilities.*
—Robert Conklin

*Next to excellence, comes the appreciation of it.*
—William Makepeace Thackeray

*I consider my ability to arouse enthusiasm among men the greatest asset I possess. The way to develop the best that is in a man is by appreciation and encouragement.*
—Charles Schwab

*My ability to throw a baseball was a gift—a God-given gift— and I truly am appreciative of that gift. It took me a while to figure that out and realize what a gift I had been given, and when I finally did, I dedicated myself to be the best pitcher that I possibly could be for as long as I possibly could.*
—Nolan Ryan

*Sometimes our light goes out but is blown again into flame by an encounter with another human being. Each of us owes the deepest thanks to those who have rekindled this inner light.*
—Albert Schweitzer

*Appreciation is a wonderful thing: It makes what is excellent in others belong to us as well.*
—Voltaire

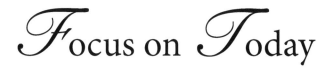

# Focus on Today

*I agree to see the best in myself and others—TODAY.*

*Become a Revolutionary Leader by practicing this Agreement, starting today—and you'll be choosing a life of empowerment for yourself and for others. Record your thoughts in your journal.*

1. List ten of your best attributes.
   *Example: Passion to serve and make a difference. Organized. Love in action. Disciplined. Honest. Loyal friend. Love to learn new ways to bring out my/our best. Strong collaborator/ cocreator. Loving wife and mother. I practice what I preach (e.g., Revolutionary Agreements).*

2. What simple steps can you take today that will empower one of your colleagues to be her or his very best?
   *Example: Change my intent: Expect to experience his magnificence.*

3. What simple steps can you take today that will empower at least one family member or friend to be their very best?
   *Example: Genuinely compliment L on the steps she is taking to strengthen her body after years of recovering from surgeries. Share my excitement about doing something active together next time she comes to visit.*

# AGREEMENT ELEVEN

# I agree to look for blessings in disguise.

*Become a possibilitarian. No matter how dark things seem to be or actually are, raise your sights and see possibilities—always see them, for they're always there.*
—Norman Vincent Peale

Have you ever been really upset with something that happened to you, only to discover later that it actually changed your life for the better? If so, you know what it is to discover a blessing in disguise. This Agreement is easy to align with when everything is going well. When a seeming catastrophe befalls us, it's not so easy.

## The Sun Behind the Cloud

When our son, Michael, was bitten by a Lyme-diseased tick in the summer of 2002, our world came to an abrupt halt. I don't think I had ever lost it as badly as I did during the months that followed.

I researched this debilitating disease day and night, joined the "Parents of Lyme Kids" Internet support group, hired and frequently spoke with four physicians from around the country, monitored the voluminous medications and immune-enhancing supplements he ingested, and even contracted for the building of a special frequency generator to aid in Michael's recovery.

Working to cope with Michael's acute illness kept me exceedingly busy, but my emotions would not stay contained. My anxiety ran rampant. I frequently broke down and wept with anguish, fear, frustration, and exhaustion. Finally, I sought out spiritual and emotional help.

During a session with my counselor, David, I let it all out. I sobbed and screamed at the top of my lungs, "This is the worst nightmare a mother could have! Not even that her child would die, but that he would suffer terribly every day for the rest of his life!" David helped me release my feelings that I was entirely responsible for Michael's well-being and that I was the only one who could help him find the way to recovery. David helped me to reconnect to the Source of Life, to know that Michael's path was his own and that all was in perfection in the grandest scheme.[1]

From this more peaceful place, I was able to start exploring other possibilities with Michael. Instead of asking, from a victim's perspective, "Why did this happen to us?" I began to wonder, "What is the blessing in this disguise? How is this trial going to be of benefit to Michael? To me? Perhaps to all of humanity?"

While we don't yet fully know all the answers, I am convinced that for every cloud there is a silver lining, and that the blessings hidden within this very large cloud must be very large and brilliant indeed.

Michael recovered completely after we discovered a frequency generator that literally burst the Lyme bacteria. Shortly after his recovery, I suggested to twelve-year-old Michael, "Because you understand this disease, perhaps you'll be able to help another child recognize it sooner—and even help save his life." So many people are misdiagnosed with everything from multiple sclerosis to rheumatoid arthritis to chronic fatigue syndrome and fibromyalgia, only to discover years later that they are afflicted with Lyme disease—and that it has now gone so deeply into every system of the body that it is far more complicated and difficult to treat.

I occasionally reflect upon Michael's experiences with the life-enhancing power of nutrition and the subtle energy of electromagnetics, which taught him to expand his thinking beyond Western medical practices and to embrace the findings of other cultures and innovators. In considering possible blessings in disguise, I thought perhaps Michael might someday engage in a holistic health care practice and save lives with his special passion. Now almost fourteen years after his recovery, Michael is thinking about applying to a progressive medical school.

## How Will It Turn Out?

Think back to one of the worst incidents in your life. Can you find any good that came from it? With practice, you will begin to identify all the positive outcomes that ultimately grow out of even seemingly horrendous circumstances. This attunes us to be alert to such future possibilities, even while in the midst of calamity.

Looking back on my divorce, it would be easy to remember the pain and anguish. But going through this experience also helped me clarify what I *did* want in my life, possibly in a way that would not have otherwise occurred. On the day that I told my former husband of my decision to divorce, I told him precisely what I wanted in my life that I felt I could not have with him. Because my emotions were so intense and I was so clear about my choices for the future, I attracted that future to me. A year later I was with Glenn, with whom I have since fulfilled my heart's desire for more than thirty years.

At the age of thirty-nine, six years after Glenn and I married, I gave birth to Michael. Although I had been healthy and strong before and through my pregnancy, for three years after Michael's birth I felt physically exhausted and battled with seemingly endless respiratory challenges. At the time, I had not yet trained myself to look for the blessing in the midst of disappointment and difficulty. I never had the thought, "I wonder what the silver lining is?" However, I would soon find the answer anyway.

As I sought desperately to regain my health and strength, a friend introduced me to a line of nutrients that seemed to give my body just what it needed. Eight months later, my friend Gail and I decided to tell everyone we knew about these life-enhancing nutrients. We hung out our shingle, and for many ensuing years enjoyed building a successful network marketing business, which I never would have considered if I hadn't needed help with my own health. The blessing extends far beyond this satisfying business venture. It also encompasses lifelong friendships developed through this work and years of residual income as a reward for helping so many others.

> *Returning to the states I found that the job I thought was waiting for me at Stanford was gone. Instead of succumbing to a feeling of defeat, I looked for the blessing in disguise. Eventually, my blessing revealed itself in a new and exciting business opportunity AND introduced me to the man who would become the love of my life.*
> *—Josephine*

## Trust the Process

In this parable from Lin Yutang's *The Importance of Living*, the old man exemplifies someone who has mastered the wisdom of this Agreement.

An Old Man was living with his son at an abandoned fort on the top of a hill, and one day he lost a horse. The neighbors came to express their sympathy for this misfortune, and the Old Man asked, "How do you know this is bad luck?" A few days afterwards, his horse returned with a number of wild horses, and when his neighbors came again to congratulate him on this stroke of good fortune, the Old Man replies, "How do you know this is good luck?" With so many horses around, his son began to take to riding, and one day he broke his leg. Again the neighbors came around to express their sympathy, and the Old Man replied, "How do you know this is bad luck?" The next year, there was a war, and because the Old Man's son was crippled, he did not have to go to the front.[2]

Sometimes, as in my years of postnatal malaise and the birth of our networking business, we are in a position to turn lemons into lemonade that we can clearly see and taste. It's great when that happens, when we can turn a lousy situation into a positive one. Often, though, it's not so easy to see or understand the outcome. We simply have to deal with the present conditions and, as my friend Joanne says, "Trust the process."

As he emerged in a weakened state from his struggles with Lyme disease, Michael reentered the world of gymnastics that had been an integral part of his life since the age of two. Despite having missed four months of practice, he decided to begin competing. We were all thrilled he felt well enough to get back in action, which blinded us to the fact that it was premature and dangerous. His lack of conditioning and confidence turned into a nightmare when he fell from the still rings, upside down, onto his head and neck.

He was paralyzed—not physically, but from the fear of breaking his neck. Only two years earlier, after missing the state overall championship by only one-twentieth of a point, Michael had held aspirations of advancing to the Olympics. After this accident, Michael never fully returned to competitive gymnastics.

Seems pretty dismal, doesn't it? So what's the upside? About a year after his last gymnastics competition, I was writing the first edition of *Revolutionary Agreements*. When it was time for me to reflect on this Agreement, I asked Michael, "Was there anything good that came out of your not returning to gymnastics?" He immediately snapped, "No!" I prodded him to consider it more carefully. He thought for a moment, then said slowly in his deep, maturing voice, "Well, karate." He enjoyed learning karate and for the many years he practiced at the gym four nights a week and competed on Saturdays, he had had no time for any other sport.

"What else?" I asked. "Civil Air Patrol," he answered with a twinkle in his eye. "I *really* like Civil Air Patrol!" (It met on Thursday nights, which had been a key gymnastics practice night.)

Looking back twelve years later, it is easy to see the blessings in disguise. Because of his engagement in Civil Air Patrol, Michael became a certified First Responder and then a volunteer firefighter and EMT. While still in high school, he was first on scene in his school's hallway to help a girl who had just been stabbed by a boy with a pair of scissors. Since then he has rescued lost hikers, extracted people from rolled-over cars, and worked in the ER as a critical care tech. One year, he received a commendation from the United States Air Force for leading the best search and rescue team in Colorado. Perhaps most significantly, he earned the position of Cadet Commander and was invited to lead his Civil Air Patrol squadron for four years, learning leadership skills that will continue to serve him and others for a lifetime. He would never have had these same opportunities if he had continued to practice gymnastics nearly every day of his young life.

*I had finished my coursework to be a certified addiction counselor. All the paperwork was in order and had been filed, and I was told I would have the certification within a few weeks. Yet, eight months later I am still waiting. I have been frustrated and angry. It is particularly difficult because it affects my pay and my ability to move to the next certification level. I could say I have learned patience, but not really. I'm usually a patient person. If I were to look for the blessing in disguise, it would be this: that I have come to understand my own worth at a deeper level. If I had gotten the letters next to my name right away, with the certification coming through as promised, I would have thought that was what made me worthwhile. Now I know I don't need that to have worth. It will be good when it comes, but my self-worth is not dependent on having letters next to my name.*

—Jessica

At a deep level, we can know that everything is unfolding as it should, evolving as it will without our interference. If we look for silver linings, blessings in disguise, we will develop the habit of finding them. If we do this enough, we can even train ourselves so that when we are actually *in the midst of* a challenging situation, we can find some peace in the moment. We can learn to see through the pain, and live in the blessing—in the light of the sun behind the cloud.

# Words of Wisdom

*"I agree to look for blessings in disguise."*

*Every exit is an entry somewhere else.*
—Tom Stoppard

*A stumbling block to the pessimist is a stepping-stone
to the optimist.*
—Eleanor Roosevelt

*I am responsible. Although I may not be able to prevent the
worst from happening, I am responsible for my attitude
toward the inevitable misfortunes that darken life. Bad things
do happen; how I respond to them defines my character
and the quality of my life. I can choose to sit in perpetual
sadness, immobilized by the gravity of my loss, or I can
choose to rise from the pain and treasure the most
precious gift I have—life itself.*
—Walter Anderson

*I thank fate for having made me born poor. Poverty taught me
the true value of the gifts useful to life.*
—Anatole France

*God turns you from one feeling to another and teaches by means
of opposites, so that you will have two wings to fly, not one.*
—Rumi

*If you are distressed by anything external, the pain is not due
to the thing itself but to your own estimate of it; and this
you have the power to revoke at any moment.*
—Marcus Aurelius

*Let us learn to appreciate there will be times when the trees
will be bare, and look forward to the time when we may
pick the fruit.*
—Anton Chekhov

*I thank Thee, first, because I was never robbed before; second,
because although they took my purse they did not take my life;
third, because although they took my all, it was not much; and
fourth because it was I who was robbed, and not I who robbed.*
—Matthew Henry

*Both abundance and lack exist simultaneously in our lives,
as parallel realities. It is always our conscious choice which
secret garden we will tend . . . when we choose not to focus
on what is missing from our lives but are grateful for the
abundance that's present—love, health, family, friends, work,
the joys of nature, and personal pursuits that bring us
pleasure—the wasteland of illusion falls away and
we experience Heaven on earth.*
—Sarah Ban Breathnach

*Some folks go through life pleased that the glass is half full.
Others spend a lifetime lamenting that it's half empty.
The truth is: There is a glass with a certain volume of
liquid in it. From there, it's up to you!*
—Dr. James S. Vuocolo

# Focus on Today

*I agree to look for blessings in disguise—TODAY.*

*Practice identifying possible positive outcomes of seemingly negative occurrences in your life. This will give you practice transforming times of struggle into realizing blessings in your life. Record your thoughts in your journal.*

1. What were some seemingly negative happenings from your past and blessings associated with those events?
   *Example: My father died.*
   *Blessing: Once my mom was unburdened of her role as caregiver, I got to really know and like her for the first time.*

   *Example: My two-year consulting contract ended and I'd done no marketing to find my next contract. I was without work.*
   *Blessing: I was now free to respond to a friend's plea for help on a project that turned into my life's passion and next vocation.*

2. What are some of your negative thoughts about current circumstances in your life? Using your imagination, what are some possible blessings in disguise corresponding to each of these negative thoughts?
   *Example: The last printing of* Revolutionary Agreements *is going to run out sooner than I had anticipated.*
   *Blessing: When I asked myself, "What should I do?" the answer was, "It's time to update the book with my new thoughts and experiences." Thus this second edition was conceived!*

# $\mathcal{A}$GREEMENT TWELVE

# I agree to lighten up!

*Once you can accept the universe as matter expanding*
*into nothing that is something, wearing stripes*
*with plaid comes easy.*
—Albert Einstein

My father used to say, "Who's responsible for you having a good time at the party?" *I am*, came the answer that I learned from an early age; *only me*. Not the host or hostess, not the music or the guests, not the food or the games. No matter what's going on, I am the only one who has the power to make me enjoy myself (or not).

Our whole life is like one big party—and my father's rule applies here too.

If you're waiting for your significant other to create joy in your relationship, give it up.

If you're waiting for things to get better at work so you can enjoy your job more, give it up.

Indeed, if you're waiting for *anything* to happen or change or improve before you can start to enjoy your life, *give it up*. It's time for a revolution!

Remember how we opened our discussion of the very first Agreement? "Someday, when I have the time . . ."?

If you notice yourself heaving a heavy sigh and thinking, "When the kids go off to college . . ." "When I get my raise . . ." "When we move . . ." "When I get married . . ." "When I get my braces off . . ." "When I lose weight . . ."—give it up, let it go, free yourself from the "*someday* . . ." trap.

This may be the last Agreement, but there's no reason you can't implement it first, immediately, right now, this very minute! Make a declaration: *No more "someday"!*

Stop waiting and live a positive life. Stop waiting and *give* to life. Become a Revolutionary Leader—show the world how to create joy in every moment.

And *enjoy* the moment. Each and every moment. After all, the moment is going to be here no matter what. Would you rather suffer through it or enjoy it? It's nothing but a choice, and it's a choice that can change your life. A choice that can change your world.

*Lighten Up!* Smile. Laugh. Love. It's good for your health. And for the health of those around you!

*As I sat feeling depressed, my eyes drifted down to the last Agreement, Lighten up! I suddenly laughed to myself thinking, "Oh, Marian, your Agreements have brought me full circle." Rather than chastise myself for what I did not do, I acknowledged myself for all that I have done and was grateful for the ability to choose what I do next. And I choose to have fun working within our community, building avenues of better communication and understanding, honoring differences, and bridging the gap of separateness that keeps us from wholeness.*

*I keep a poster of the Agreements in my office as a reminder of what is available to me every day and when*

*people look at them and ask, "What are those, Dan?" I say,*
*"Well, I am so glad you asked. Got a few minutes?"*
      *—Dan*

# A Reverse Epiphany

As I disembarked from a plane in Miami after an unusually bumpy flight, I had a sort of reverse epiphany. Suddenly, circumstances seemed as far from *light* as they could be.

I was still on edge from the rough flight. The airport was jammed, the heat was sweltering, people were exhaling nicotine and tar at me, the smog was thick, all around me people were complaining loudly and grumpily, and to top it all off, my ride was late. Everything about my situation felt heavy, dark, glum, and in every way the *opposite* of "light."

It was a moment of endarkenment!

I forced myself to direct my own pontification at myself, remembering my words, "There's always something to enjoy about the moment . . ." And I began to laugh out loud, because I could not find *one single thing* to enjoy about this moment—not one! All at once the absurdity of the situation struck me, which made me laugh even more: *I was enjoying the fact that I couldn't find a single thing to enjoy!*

"Why not laugh at the absurdity of life?" I asked myself. And so I did. Miraculously, my stress lifted and I felt lighter. Could it be that simple? Well, yes.

According to the Association for Applied and Therapeutic Humor, laughter has been, "scientifically proven to reduce pain, strengthen our immune system, decrease stress, lower blood pressure while improving circulation, help us put life's trials and tribulations into healthy perspective by making them seem less significant, aid us in overcoming fear, allow us to take ourselves less seriously, and trigger our creativity."[1]

If your situation is more dire than my mere traveling experience and it's hard to figure out how to get from despair to laughter, you might consult the work of Norman Cousins who turned his ill health around with laughter. He discovered that just ten minutes of belly laughter while watching funny films would give him two hours of pain free sleep without taking painkillers.[2] In those days, he needed to rent films. Today it's as simple as searching the Internet for funny videos on any subject that makes you smile. Among my favorites are funny animal and baby videos, and the contagious laughter from "laughing" YouTube videos.

## Lighten Up at Work

I recall certain "lighten up" moments from decades ago as though they just happened yesterday. Two of them occurred while working as the Manager for Educational Development at the US Senate.

My boss Mary Ruth and I were sitting facing each other, knee to knee (and almost nose to nose), quietly discussing a serious personnel issue. The situation weighed heavily on us both. I took a deep breath and looked into her eyes. Suddenly my heart opened and I saw myself from a higher vantage point. Laughter bubbled up and I could hardly believe the words that emerged from my mouth. "This is fun!" I said. She smiled. The drama of the situation transformed into an engaging puzzle to solve together. In a flash of "lightening up" my mood changed and my creativity was released for the good.

At another time, I found myself complaining bitterly to one of my leaders about a work situation. Instead of going down the path of negativity with me, Bob surprised me by smiling in response and saying, "You love your job, don't you?!" I experienced an instant state shift, from the dark drama I was creating to the joy that was the truth he so astutely named.

What Bob did for me that day was revolutionary. By seeing the best in me and shining the light on the positive, he gave me a gift that continues to serve me many years later. Often when I catch myself in a downward drama spiral, his wise words return to remind me we can choose to focus on the light instead of the darkness. It's amazing to me that one little statement we make to someone can change that person's life. And this applies equally to negative and positive statements.

*One day, in the midst of a particularly packed schedule of back-to-back meetings and deadlines, I was checking my iPhone calendar, my computer calendar, and my Day-Timer trying to make sure I wasn't going to miss any appointments or overlook something important. My cell phone rang. I noticed it was my son calling, and he rarely contacts me by phone. My heart sank as I anxiously answered. "Hi, Mom," he said. "Levi wants to say something to you." Levi, my grandson, was just learning to talk the last time I had seen him, so I had never talked with him on the phone.*

*"Hi Oma," he said, clear as a bell. "I just pooped in the potty."*

*It certainly put it all in perspective. Perhaps it was God again, calling to say, "Martie, lighten up!"* [3]
*—Martie*

## Creating Our Reality

Having just been interviewed on the Sterling Spin radio show, I stayed on the line to listen to the next guest, Dianne Collins, author of *Do You QuantumThink?* What I learned in the first minutes of her interview was highly instructive.

Dianne revealed that when the show host had called her that morning and asked her the usual, "How are you?" Dianne's mind immediately went to the challenging morning she had with her husband. In an instant she recognized that she could *report* on what had happened or she could *create* a new reality in that very moment. She chose the latter and responded, "Fabulous!"

The radio show host seemed stunned by Dianne's disclosure and said, "I can't believe you were anything but fabulous when you answered my question, Dianne. In fact, the energy I felt from you when you said 'Fabulous!' started my day out great."

"That's because I *did* feel fabulous," said Dianne. "I created it in that very moment."

What if we applied QuantumThinking throughout our day by consciously choosing our intent and then allowing it to unfold? The mission you created or reinforced in Agreement One serves as one of your intents. What other intents do you consciously— or unconsciously—carry in your thoughts each day?

I am inspired by my friend Vivian's intent, which is her stated mission: *To make a positive difference in the life of everybody I meet.*

When I go about my day with this thought in mind, I am amazed at the difference in my interactions. I am aware that I smile at people more, naturally tap more into my inner joy, and feel more connected to others. I invite you to join me in doing this for just one hour. (Perhaps that hour will extend to the rest of your life!)

## Discovering Now

In 2000, I lost my joy. I went looking for it everywhere: in my relationship with my husband; in satisfaction stemming from my work; in my connection with Spirit. I spent hours and hours in the mountains every week, hoping that by communing with Nature I would find the answer.

I asked, "What am I to do next? Please show me the way! There must be more to life than this. I am almost fifty years old and I have not yet saved the world. I know I'm here for a greater purpose, and I am ready to *get on* with it! What should I do?!"

No answers came. At least, not the ones I wanted to hear. All I heard was: "It's not what you do, it's how you do it. Do whatever you like." Well, I didn't know what I liked.

I searched all year. I read personal growth books and attended course after course, seeking the answer. And then, *Bingo!* I found it. It was something I had already known, but only intellectually. Suddenly it became as real to me as my skin.

*Be here now.* Simple . . . right?

*Be here now.* "What do you mean?" I asked the still, small voice inside me. "Where else would I be?" But even as I asked, I knew the answer. I would be somewhere else. Or more accurately, some *when* else. My mind was often away from *now*, mulling over some past event or worrying obsessively over some imagined future. I looked like I was here, all the lights were on, the car was in the driveway . . . but my mind had snuck away to fret.

*Be here now.* All at once I got it, and my negative emotions vanished. They had to—there simply was no room for them in the *now.* My negative thoughts and emotions all seemed to be related to something that happened in a remembered past or an imagined future. But they weren't real any longer. In fact, they never really had been.

There was only, always, *now.*

After leaving my job of nine years at the US Senate to move to Colorado and join my husband's consulting firm, my friend

Trish would call me from DC with worry in her voice. "How are you doing, Marian? Are you doing okay financially?" After lamenting about the uncertainties of my new life, I would inevitably say, "If you took a snapshot of me at any moment in time, my life would look great." This statement revealed my budding recognition of the perfection of each moment, even though I worried incessantly about the future, or uncomfortably replayed what happened to me yesterday.

My upbringing in the Jewish tradition of suffering had its impact on me. For years, asking my mother, "How are you?" invariably resulted in her wincing as she replied with an elongated sigh, "Okay ..."—even if she was having the best day of her life. We were taught to suffer, to remember the atrocities that befell our people. Our mothers, aunts, and grandmothers modeled how to be martyrs, to sacrifice personal desire for the good of the family. "I'll take the shriveled up piece of meat. Here, you have the tender one." It was rare to find a matriarch in our family who expressed feeling really good, happy, and content. I had no female role models to show me how to lighten up.

When I make the shift to now, releasing yesterday and tomorrow, drama and suffering vanish and ease sets in.

The original Geneva Group Agreement for "lighten up" is "I agree to create joy in my relationships, my work, and my life." I learned to do this simply by being present. By living "in the moment." And it is *good*. In fact, it is more than good. In the stillness of every moment, I discovered I could find peace. Joy. Bliss. Ecstasy. Love beyond the ability of any words to fully convey.

On the outside, my life looked the same. I didn't change my work, my relationships, my hair color, my name, nor anything else visible. But my life began being *filled* with joyful moments.

I created a new intent, which I shared with you as one of my stated missions in Agreement One: *To fully enjoy life and experience love in every moment.* To fulfill this intent, I have become very clear about the people I choose to spend my time with. In the "I Choose..." section that follows, I list the attributes of those who I'd like to show up in my life—and as a result, they do.

Would you rather be surrounded by loving, aware people who are enjoying their lives? Or by people who fairly consistently choose to suffer? (Remember, like attracts like; misery loves company.) How do you want to live your life? As poet Mary Oliver inquires, "Tell me, what is it you plan to do with your one wild and precious life?"

I hope it is to join me as a Revolutionary Leader. To be the light that you truly are. To exude the joy that is your birthright. To laugh unabashedly and bring laughter to others. To create joy in your relationships, your work, and your life.

*Lighten Up!* In so doing, you light up the world!

# Words of Wisdom

*"I agree to lighten up!"*

*My mission is to make a positive difference in the life of everybody I meet.*
—Vivian Saccucci

*If it's true that we are here to help others, then what exactly are the others here for?*
—author unknown

*Life loves to be taken by the lapel and told, "I'm with you kid. Let's go."*
—Maya Angelou

*If we don't make some changes, the status quo will remain the same.*
—generally attributed to a member of President Bill Clinton's staff

*Change is inevitable, except from a vending machine.*
—Robert C. Gallagher

*Despite the cost of living, have you noticed how it remains so popular?*
—author unknown

*God put me on earth to accomplish a certain number of things.*
*Right now I am so far behind, I will live forever.*
—author unknown

*Don't worry about the world coming to an end today.*
*It is already tomorrow in Australia.*
—Charles M. Schulz

*"If you light a lamp for somebody, it will also brighten your path."*
– Buddha

*Experience is something you don't get until just after you need it.*
—Sir Laurence Olivier

*If you try to fail, and succeed, which have you done?*
—Steven Wright

*And forget not that the earth delights to feel your bare feet and*
*the winds long to play with your hair.*
—Kahlil Gibran

*I plan on living forever. So far, so good.*
— Steven Wright

*i thank You God for most this amazing day;*
*for the leaping greenly spirits of trees,*
*and a blue true dream of sky;*
*and for everything which is natural which is infinite which is yes.*
—e.e. cummings

# ℱocus on ℐoday

*I agree to lighten up!—TODAY.*

*Agreement One ("I agree to live my mission") encouraged you to identify what you really want—and then to live it. We've come full circle. With this Agreement, you commit to live your life in joy. Record your thoughts in your journal.*

1.  Review your mission statement from Agreement One. Rewrite it (or change it, if appropriate) and add words like "enjoy," "joy" or "joyfully" if they are not already in it: *Example: I joyfully facilitate the alignment of leaders.*

2.  Ask yourself, "What one small thing will I do *today* to lighten up?" *Example: Call a friend and share something fun with her.*

3.  What has happened as a result of doing that one small thing? *Example: I shared something special that's occurring with my son. She was so happy for him and me! Then she shared something special that just happened yesterday for her daughter. We both laughed and enjoyed this heart-opening experience.*

# $\mathcal{I}$ Choose…

*The best way to predict your future is to create it.*
—Abraham Lincoln

The future is now. You are creating it in this very moment. What do you choose?

*I* choose to surround myself with like-minded, light-hearted friends.

I choose to surround myself with:

*People who are passionate about living their missions and who support one another to achieve their goals and dreams;*

*People I can trust to always speak their truth with compassion for themselves and others;*

*People who look within themselves for clues to learning and transformation when emotions flare;*

*People who are open to continuously choosing and re-choosing what works and changing what doesn't;*

*People who listen with their hearts rather than imposing their own needs or interpretations on what others say;*

*People who respect my right to my own perspective and who honor our diverse choices;*

*People I can trust to always take problems directly to the source (especially if it's me), and who will remind me to do the same;*

*People who acknowledge me for the contributions I make and graciously accept my acknowledgment of them;*

*People who see the best in themselves and others, and who expect the best from their circumstances;*

*People who feel gratitude for the blessings in their life, even before the blessings may be obvious;*

*People with whom I can effortlessly lighten up and feel completely free!*

Simply put, I choose to surround myself with people who embrace the principles behind these Revolutionary Agreements as a guide to creating a positive life. I invite you to join me!

# CREATING A POSITIVE WORLD

Perhaps you are thinking, "This all sounds good and makes sense to me as I read it, but how do I keep it alive, as a real ongoing experience in my everyday life? Not just today and tomorrow, but next week, next month, next year?"

## Use this book

One answer, of course, is to do what we always do with books that hold special meaning for us—highlight passages we want to remember, make notes in the margins, read and reread. Reading one Agreement just before sleep or first thing in the morning upon awakening is another great way to imprint the material more deeply in your consciousness.

> *I bought the poster of the Agreements and mounted it on the ceiling above my bed so that I could see them first thing in the morning and last thing at night.*
> *—Bonnie*

Consider focusing on one of the twelve Revolutionary Agreements each month for a year. Repeat that Agreement's "Focus on Today" exercise every day or once a week during that month until each Agreement has become such an intrinsic part of you that its daily practice comes naturally, effortlessly, and joyfully.

## Join or Create a Practice Group

To deepen your experience of these Agreements (and begin to transform your world as a result), consider becoming part of a practice group that nurtures these ideas as a tangible reality in your everyday lives. This is exactly what Glenn and I did in 1985 with about a dozen friends and colleagues when we cocreated the Geneva Group. This forum met monthly for twenty years to support like-minded, like-hearted souls in our mission:

> *To develop and maximize our personal growth and evolution, thus enhancing our relationships and all life on the planet through reflecting unconditional love, support, and well-being.*

To start your own group, simply share this book with a few friends, people you care about. Ask them if they'd like to start a practice group around the Revolutionary Agreements. Choose a time when you can gather uninterrupted. One very practical way to use this time together is to devote each session to discussing and sharing your experiences with a single Agreement. If you are a coach, facilitator, or consultant and feel inspired to add Revolutionary Agreements programs and coaching to your offerings, you may choose to become a Certified Revolutionary Agreements Coach. Visit http://www.agreementsinstitute.com to learn more.

Connect with a worldwide community of people using these Agreements who are committed to cocreating a positive future. Participate in or initiate a conversation at your favorite social media site.

## Guidelines for Practice Group Gatherings

When you meet in person, use the first few minutes of your session to come together and establish your sense of being present with one another. We often began Geneva Group gatherings by playing uplifting music in the background while we connected with each other in silence. It's amazing how much more deeply we can connect when we're not talking. Some people reach out to touch another's hand, others embrace their friends with a hug, still others share an authentic, welcoming smile. Mostly we'd simply reconnect by witnessing the joy in each other's eyes as we looked through the windows to the soul.

You will find your own ways to connect. If you're not quite comfortable with or ready for the intimacy of silent greetings, you might start with a simple check-in process. Sitting in a circle, ask each person to complete this phrase however he or she likes, "What I feel like saying is . . ." Each person in turn completes this phrase to let everyone else know how they're doing in just a few words, and to help release any thoughts that might keep them from being completely present with the group.

Continue this around the circle as many times as is necessary for each person to feel ready to participate fully. When the opportunity to speak comes around, anyone can conclude their own check-in by simply saying, "I'm present." When everyone has said, "I'm present," you're ready to move on. It is easy to adapt this type of check-in to a group that meets by phone or virtually.

However you elect to begin, it's a good idea to identify a specific process and not just "wing it." Rituals help us to connect with each other and ground us in the essence of this work. Opening with a silent greeting or a verbal check-in are rituals. A short invocation, meditation, or prayer can be a ritual. As an example, "Guide us to know the depth of the meaning behind these Agreements, that we may create peace in our lives and Peace on Earth."

From this place of quieted mind, one person reads your group's mission, if you have one. For example, "Our mission is to support each other in effectively using the Revolutionary

213

Agreements to live positive lives and together create a positive future for all." Each person in turn then reads one of the Agreements aloud, until all twelve have been recited.

Explore the Agreement you've chosen for that gathering. Each is multifaceted like a sparkling diamond, a reflection of who you are and who you choose to become. Let yourself fully explore the potential of living this Agreement. Allow yourself to go to places in your mind and heart where you may not have previously traveled.

Share your experiences with each other of how practicing these Agreements at home, at work, and in your world is affecting your life. Be good listeners for each other, allowing each person to be fully heard. Problem-solve only if requested by the speaker.

End each gathering with a round of, "What I feel like saying is . . ." When the opportunity to speak comes around, anyone can conclude their sharing by simply saying, "I'm complete."

If no one in your group is a Certified Revolutionary Agreements Coach, consider inviting all members of the group to facilitate a regularly scheduled gathering so that you take turns leading and no one person is burdened with the role of organizer and facilitator. The greater the participation, the greater the reward.

## Revolutionary Agreements in the Workplace

You may want to introduce these Agreements in your various spheres of influence. Your family, neighborhood group, congregation, and service organizations may be appropriate and fruitful places to do this. A free Facilitator's Guide is available for congregations.[1]

Many work teams have used these Agreements as a basis for supporting their organization's mission and enhancing communication skills. You will find several examples of organizations' customized Agreements in the upcoming "Personalized Agreements" section.

Some organizations have used the Agreements as the foundation for comprehensive training. Others simply read each Agreement aloud in turn at the beginning of each staff meeting to help align the team and set the tone for honest communication. Yet other organizations progress through the Agreements by choosing one to focus on for a week or a month, then moving on to each of the others in turn.

The potential impact of these Agreements in the place where many of us spend much of our lives—our places of work—is tremendous. Imagine the positive changes that would occur if your peers, supervisors, and staff followed the principles of Truth, Acceptance, and Gratitude that lie at the heart of the Revolutionary Agreements. Further, imagine the ripple effects if you and your colleagues brought these Agreements home and into your communities at large, so that what you learn and practice in the workplace infuses your interactions with *everyone*.

## Transforming the World

In *The Tipping Point: How Little Things Can Make a Big Difference*, Malcolm Gladwell explains how small groups of influential individuals play a critical role in creating mass consciousness. "It's easier to remember and appreciate something, after all, if you discuss it for two hours with your best friends. . . . Small, close-knit groups have the power to magnify the epidemic potential of a message or idea."[2]

As Revolutionary Leaders, we have just such a "message with epidemic potential." We choose to promote a new way of thinking, to live positive lives, to dare to think and act in such a way that we change a world of negativity, fear, and contraction to one of positivity, love, and expansion.

As a Revolutionary Leader, my personal mission is to foster an environment of genuine collaboration in which we can all express our unique creativity and fulfill our collective potential for good.

It is clear to me that a sweeping, worldwide change, from a fear-based to a love-based existence, is only an evolutionary step away. We can make the choice to join together and speed up this natural next phase of our development by adopting these Agreements as our way of life—and in so doing, move into the fullness of our truth as loving beings, fueled by the Divine spark of life.

My deepest desire is that you join me in this Revolution by helping to create a tidal wave of powerful, positive, and enduring impact on our world. If this sounds ambitious, remember this: throughout history, it is individuals, caught up in the impassioned grip of an idea whose time has come, who have always created the most lasting, positive impact. These times call for Revolutionary Agreements.

As Margaret Mead expressed so beautifully in her oft-quoted statement, "Never doubt that a small group of thoughtful, committed citizens can change the world. Indeed, it is the only thing that ever has."[3]

Join me by adopting conscious Agreements for living a positive life and embodying Gandhi's challenge to "be the change you wish to see in the world." When we are living the authentic Love that we are (Truth), when we have released the shackles of judgment (Acceptance), and when we unceasingly see and feel the grace in our lives (Gratitude), we will enjoy peace in our hearts and together create Peace on Earth.

# $\mathscr{P}$ERSONALIZED AGREEMENTS

The Revolutionary Agreements are based upon twenty years of using and exploring the impact of the Geneva Group Agreements on the lives and communities of about fifty friends and colleagues. The Geneva Group Agreements rightly lead off this section.

Some Geneva Group participants and their friends, along with some readers of the first edition of *Revolutionary Agreements*, have personalized the Agreements for their work and home communities.

One Geneva Group member created a powerful process to guide corporate and nonprofit teams in developing their own Agreements.

On the following pages, you will find a sampling of personalized and customized Agreements. Feel free to draw from any of these that serve you in creating greater peace in your life and world. Acknowledging the source is appreciated.

Please share with me (via email at marian @revolutionaryagreements.com) any Agreements you create for use at your home or work so we may add them as a resource to others at http://www.revolutionarychoices.com and associated social media sites.

# Where It All Began:
# Geneva Group Agreements

At its first gathering in June 1985, Geneva Group participants began to develop Agreements that would guide us in living our highest values in all aspects of our lives. At the start of each subsequent Geneva Group gathering, participants read each of the Agreements aloud in turn. We then would reflect on the positive impact of the Agreements on our families, coworkers, clients, and communities.

As the Geneva Group and its participants evolved over the subsequent twenty years of monthly meetings, so did the Agreements. I have included two versions of the Geneva Group Agreements: the initial Agreements (called Ground Rules), followed by the current version of the Geneva Group Agreements.

## Geneva Group – Ground Rules (June 1985)

1. I agree to support the vision and purpose of the organization and to use the vision and purpose as a guide to my actions.
2. I agree to be honest, thorough and responsible in my communications.
3. I agree to respectfully receive the communications of others.
4. I agree to do whatever it takes to get the job done, including doing someone else's job when necessary.
5. I agree to look for opportunities to learn from my experiences, to continue doing what works and discontinue doing what does not work.
6. I agree to be open to new business strategies.
7. I agree to clean up any damage I create between myself and others in personal interactions.
8. I agree to come from a sense of caring and connectedness in my interactions with others.
9. I agree to acknowledge others for what they have either done or not done.
10. I agree to be responsible for getting acknowledged.
11. I agree to support others and to be supported in participating at the highest level of excellence.
12. I agree to offer at least one solution any time I present a problem.

13. I agree to take problems, complaints, and upsets to someone who can do something about it. I agree not to criticize or complain to someone who cannot do something about my complaint, and I will redirect others to do the same.
14. I agree to acknowledge that everyone, including myself, is making the absolute best choice or decision they are capable of at the moment of choice or decision.
15. I agree to continually choose and re-choose to be in this organization.

## Geneva Group Agreements (July 2015)

1. Committing to the Mission:
   I agree to use the mission of Geneva Group, and the following agreements, as a guide to my actions.

2. Communicating with Integrity:
   I agree to tell my truth, with compassion for myself and others.

3. Listening with Heart:
   I agree to listen respectfully to the communication of others and attune to their deepest meaning.

4. Honoring One Another:
   I agree to honor each person's process, acknowledging that everyone, including myself, is making the best possible choice or decision we are capable of at that moment of choice or decision.

5. Appreciating One's Self:
   I agree to take responsibility for acknowledging myself and receiving acknowledgement from others.

6. Expressing Appreciation:
   I agree to acknowledge others.

7. Honoring Differences:
   I agree to come from a sense of cooperation and caring in my interactions with others, and from an understanding that goals are often the same even though methods for achieving them may differ.

8. Using Grievances as Opportunities:
   I agree to look for the unresolved issue within me that creates a disproportionate reaction to another's behavior.

9. Maintaining Harmony:
   I agree to take the time to establish rapport and then to re-connect with anyone with whom I feel out of harmony as soon as it's appropriate.

10. Resolving Problems Constructively:
    I agree to take problems, complaints and upsets to the person(s) with whom I can resolve them, at the earliest opportunity. I agree not to criticize or complain to someone who cannot do something about my complaint, and I will recommend that others do the same.

11. Learning From Experience:
    I agree to look for opportunities to learn from my experiences, to continue doing what works and discontinue doing what does not work.

12. Going For Excellence!
    I agree to support others and to be supported in participating at the highest level of excellence.

13. Trusting the Process:
    I agree to release my judgments about the process I am in and to value the outcome as appropriate for me at the moment.

14. Being a rEvolutionary Leader:
    I agree to foster an environment of genuine collaboration, in which all people, including myself, feel empowered to express our individual and collective potential.

15. Re-evaluating Commitment:
    I agree to choose and re-choose to participate in Geneva Group. It's my choice.

16. Lightening Up!
    I agree to create fun and joy in my relationships, my work, my play, and my life.

# Corporate Team Agreements

Three sets of corporate agreements follow—from a large Fortune 50 company, a midsize company, and a sole proprietorship.

## Large Company

The Director of Systems & Development in a communications company was facing serious challenges at work. With the help of a consultant and sample agreements, he and his team spent a full day creating their own unifying agreements they termed "Our Foundation." As he later shared in our e-newsletter *Revolutionary News*, "We have been functioning as a cohesive team with our new agreements for seven months now and to say that this core organization has turned itself around would be an understatement." (Full story can be found at http://www.revolutionarychoices.com/results.)

### OUR FOUNDATION: TO THIS WE AGREE . . .

**Keep Things in Their Proper Perspective.** I agree to create joy in my relationships, my work, my life, and to appreciate the humor in our daily lives.

**Keep Commitments.** I agree to only make commitments I am willing and able to keep. I will consider whether I have the authority, information, tools, time, and support to do what is being requested and will make certain my needs are heard and understood. I will renegotiate commitments as appropriate and necessary.

**Go For Excellence.** I agree to support others and to be supported in participating at the highest level of excellence, enabling a positive internal and external customer experience.

**Respect.** I agree to treat others with mutual respect and professionalism. I will operate from a sense of cooperation, respect, caring, and support in my interactions with others, understanding that goals are often the same although methods of accomplishing them may differ.

**Appreciate My Contributions.** I agree to take responsibility for acknowledging myself and receiving acknowledgement from others.

**Express Appreciation for Others' Contributions.** I agree to acknowledge others and celebrate team accomplishments as well. I will work to create an environment that supports independent decision-making and risk-taking when appropriate.

**Focus on the Future, Grow from Experience.** I agree to let the past be the past and to work as a team for the future.

**Seek Advice from Others.** I agree to ask for advice from others and to listen to the advice that is offered.

**Tell the Truth with Compassion and Candor.** I agree to take the responsibility to communicate openly and honestly, focusing on the issue or behavior, not on the person.

**Resolve Conflict Constructively.** I agree to take problems, complaints, and upsets to the person(s) with whom I can resolve them, not to criticize or complain to colleagues who cannot do something about my complaint, and I will redirect others to do the same.

**Be a rEvolutionary Leader.** I agree to foster an environment of genuine collaboration, in which all people, including myself, feel empowered to express our individual and collective potential.

## Midsize Company

David Neenan, founder of the construction company that earned the Foundation for Financial Service Professionals' highly coveted American Business Ethics award in 2013, built his business on a foundation he called "Rules of the Game." Inspired by the same source that inspired the Geneva Group Agreements, the "Rules of the Game" are posted in the company's spacious break room.

### RULES OF THE GAME

**Communication:**
1. Speak with good purpose.
2. Be open, honest, and candid in your communication with others.
3. Don't shoot the messenger.
4. Make public your private concerns/conversations directly to those with whom you have the concern.
5. Listen intently to understand and address others' concerns.

**Coordinating Action:**

6. Manage your promises.
    a. Only make agreements that you intend to keep; renegotiate when you have to.
    b. Raise the flag. Clear up any broken or potentially broken agreements as soon as you become aware of them.
7. Focus on what works and declare a breakdown when it doesn't.

**Learning:**

8. It is okay if you make a mistake. Learn from it.
9. Offer negative and positive assessments in order to support learning for others and for yourself.
10. View innovation as an essential part of your job.

**Producing Value:**

11. Add value (more for less) for the customer, for TNC, and for yourself.
12. Identify and eliminate waste.
13. Be generous to the community.

**Emotional Competence:**

14. Be willing to win and allow others to win (abundance).
15. Treat others in a manner such that they feel respected and appreciated.
16. If a problem arises, look first to the system–not the people–then make the correction.
17. Maintain a sense of humor and remember to breathe.
18. Take responsibility for your own experience at The Neenan Company.

## Sole Proprietorship

Rachel Claret is the founder and operator of ORGANIZEN™. When she was only eleven years old her parents, Jon and Laurie Weiss, brought to Colorado the personal development program that inspired the creation of Geneva Group. Jon and Laurie have been at the core of the Geneva Group during its twenty years of monthly meetings, and they have contributed greatly to the development and evolution of the Geneva Group Agreements. Rachel attended gatherings as a teenager and young woman and later integrated the Agreements into her life as a mother of four, an entrepreneur, and a business owner.

## MISSION

The mission of ORGANIZEN™ is to
1. joyfully serve our clients and encourage them to experience miracles;
2. expertly train our associates, enabling them to prosper and grow;
3. handsomely reward our investors, associates, and allies; and
4. demonstrate excellence at every level.

## OPERATING AGREEMENTS

Everyone associated with the operation of ORGANIZEN™ has agreed to do their best to keep the following agreements. They are adapted from the Geneva Group Agreements, created in Boulder/Denver, Colorado (1985). If you wish, you may copy and/or amend them for your own use.

1. **Committing to the Mission:** We agree to use the mission of ORGANIZEN™ as a guide to our actions.

2. **Focusing on the Moment:** We agree to give our full attention to the task at hand and the person with whom we're communicating.

3. **Listening with Heart:** We agree to listen with our hearts to the communication of others and attune to their deepest meaning.

4. **Communicating with Integrity:** We agree to tell the truth as we see it, with compassion and integrity.

5. **Honoring One Another:** We agree to honor each person's process, acknowledging that everyone, including ourselves, is making the best possible choice or decision we are capable of at that moment of choice or decision.

6. **Appreciating Oneself:** We agree to take responsibility for acknowledging ourselves and receiving acknowledgment from others.

7. **Expressing Appreciation:** We agree to express our appreciation for others, and to acknowledge their contributions.

8. **Honoring Differences:** We agree to come from a sense of cooperation and caring in our interactions with others; and from an understanding that goals are often the same even though methods for achieving them may differ.

9. **Using Grievances as Opportunities:** We agree to look for the unresolved issue within ourselves that creates a disproportionate reaction to someone else's behavior.

10. **Maintaining Harmony:** We agree to take the time to establish rapport and then to reconnect with anyone with whom we feel out of harmony as soon as it's appropriate.

11. **Resolving Problems Constructively:** We agree to take problems, complaints, and upsets to the person(s) with whom we can resolve them, at the earliest opportunity. We agree not to criticize or complain to someone who cannot do something about our complaint, and we will recommend that others do the same.

12. **Learning from Experience:** We agree to look for opportunities to learn from our experiences, to continue doing what works and discontinue doing what does not work.

13. **Going for Excellence!** We agree to support others and to be supported in participating at the highest level of excellence.

14. **Trusting the Process:** We agree to release our judgments about the process we are in and to value the outcome as appropriate for us at the moment.

15. **Being a rEvolutionary Leader:** We agree to foster an environment of genuine collaboration, in which all people, including each of us, feel empowered to express our individual and collective potential. We agree to be leaders.

16. **Re-evaluating Commitment:** We agree to choose and re-choose to participate. It's our choice.

17. **Lightening Up!** We agree to create fun and joy in our relationships, our work, our play, and our life.

# Team Agreements for Nonprofit Organizations

Joanne Cohen is a Senior Organizational Consultant and Partner at CTAT LLC. She has designed and facilitated corporate team building, leadership development, and stress management workshops for years using the Geneva Group Agreements and other agreements developed through her "Raising the Bar" workshops.

> *When Agreements are practiced diligently, people can be more proactive and less reactive to the daily challenges inside and outside the work environment. Once we learn to communicate more effectively and manage our stressors, we are able to tap into a vast knowledge that is available to each of us; and we can express that knowing from a more powerful place. Multiply that by a whole team operating together from such a place and the possibilities are limitless.*

She describes the process and rewards of taking teams through a team building simulation/process resulting in the development of fundamental operating agreements.

> *I am well aware that most participants come to my team building sessions initially because management decrees they must. My job is to involve them in a simulation that morphs a group of colleagues into a cohesive team. In a half-, full- or two-day process, the group is presented with sample agreements created by other teams with whom I have worked, along with both the initial and current versions of the Revolutionary Agreements. With these guides the "group" becomes a "team" and recreates itself while discovering and demonstrating its teaming abilities.*
> *Working closely together, participants support each other in tearing down individual barriers and creating an item of focus*

226

*such as integrity, respect, managing conflict, teamwork, or making the workplace a place of fun (Lighten Up!). Ultimately, they design and draft a new set of agreements from which they will not only operate but for which they will hold themselves and each other accountable. We follow up with each team over six months to support them in keeping the momentum going.*

*Pride and a sense of accomplishment result from taking ownership for this process. The tremendous positive energy generated by the end of our time together is not only deeply satisfying—it inspires me to continue taking this work to others across the United States.*

*Each participant is given a copy of the book,* Revolutionary Agreements, *at the end of the session to help them reinforce the power of following agreements in their lives, both inside and outside of work.*

*As the successful teams grow in numbers, positive change occurs naturally around them. People who have engaged in the process demonstrate their success as they "become the change" they want to see.*

In 2001, Joanne guided the Center for Technical Assistance and Training (CTAT) team at Rocky Mountain Human Services to create its own set of Agreements.

*These Agreements were read at each monthly staff meeting and the team selected one per month to focus on and report about at the next meeting. In 2015, the team revisited these Agreements to determine if they were in alignment with the organization's current vision and goals. The updated Agreements are below.*

## CTAT's ANCHOR POINTS

**ACCOUNTABILITY:** I agree to take ownership and responsibility for my relationships, commitments, and projects.

**APPRECIATION:** I agree to value our differences, express appreciation and gratitude for others' contributions and celebrate personal and team accomplishments.

**COMMUNICATION:** I agree to engage in dialog with positive intention, listen openly, address concerns truthfully and compassionately, and resolve issues by offering solutions.

**CREATIVITY AND INNOVATION:** I agree to energize the creative talents in everyone and leverage our diverse strengths to develop exceptional products and services that improve and expand our revenue sources.

**EXCELLENCE:** I agree to work effectively with my team, using mistakes and challenges as opportunities to learn and grow, thereby focusing on achieving superior results that exceed customer expectations.

**RESPECT:** I agree to see the best in myself and others while being considerate, caring, and supportive, addressing concerns in a professional manner.

**STRATEGIC BUSINESS DEVELOPMENT:** I agree to create partnerships and plan projects based on capacity, revenue potential, expertise, and sustainability.

**TRUST:** I agree to fulfill my commitments with honesty, integrity, and dignity, knowing that my actions will create trust among my colleagues and customers.

**UNITED FRONT:** I agree to contribute to projects as a cohesive team member, supporting decisions and actions, while being mindful of the CTAT and RMHS mission and goals.

**WORK-LIFE HARMONY:** I agree to have fun in work and life while maintaining balance, focus, perspective, and enthusiasm.

We agree to support each other in keeping these agreements, regularly reviewing them for relevancy and importance.

# Professional Development Programs

Melisa Pearce is a Life Coach, Founder of Touched by a Horse, Inc.®, author, entrepreneur, horsewoman, national speaker, and creator of a two-year training program for her Equine Gestalt Coaching Method®.

*All my work—with clients, staff, and horses—is based on making agreements for working together. One of my women's programs is a one-year commitment to multiple transformational retreats held at various locations across the country. This is a deep discovery process that provides an opportunity for learning and positive transformation that can occur when working through personal challenges.*

*I use two sets of agreements for these retreats: one for staff (coaches, facilitators, and administration) and one for my clients to use as a working model to help develop their own agreements. Our agreements have made working together so much easier, with less struggle and difficulty among staff or with clients.*

*The following Agreements are read aloud and signed by participants at the beginning of each of the eight core trainings that comprise their certification program as well as at our annual convention where we read them out loud together. We credit the Agreements as being the covenants that keep our large community mindful of respectful connections.*

**Touched by a Horse® Certification Program Agreements**

1. **Commit to Being Present**
   I commit to the Certification Program and will focus on being fully engaged in the process.

2. **Communicate with Integrity**
   I agree to tell my truth and be open to the truth of others.
   I agree to make only agreements I am willing and able to keep.

3. **Listen Deeply**
   I agree to listen respectfully to the communication of others and to be receptive to the meaning behind the words.

4. **Honor One Another**
   I agree to speak only positively about Touched by a Horse associates, coaches, participants, and corporate staff. I agree to acknowledge that everyone, including myself, is making the best possible choice or decision we are capable of at that moment, and will presume innocence rather than assign negative motives.

5. **Take Responsibility**
   I take full responsibility for my thoughts, feelings, and actions. I use "I" statements and own my experience, respond vs. react, and question assumptions when I am unclear. I agree to acknowledge others.

6. **Appreciate the Good**
   I agree to focus first on what is working, and to acknowledge, recognize, and give thanks to others for their contributions. I agree to accept thanks and acknowledge my own contributions by celebrating successes both large and small.

7. **Honor Differences**
   I agree to come from a sense of cooperation and caring in my interactions with others, understanding that goals are often the same even though methods for achieving them may differ.

8. **Create Safe Space**
   I agree to foster an environment of genuine collaboration in which all people, including myself, feel empowered to express our individual and collective potential. I model the way through the use of empowering language choice, making effective requests and honoring my promises.

9. **Resolve Problems Constructively**
   I agree to take problems, complaints, and upsets to the person or persons with whom I can resolve them at the earliest opportunity. I agree to let go of the language of commiseration and complaint (gossip) and I will redirect others to do the same.

10. **Lighten Up and Stay Flexible**
    I agree to lighten up and have some fun, and I remain flexible and adapt to changes. I view mistakes as learning opportunities

rather than failures. I agree to create joy in my relationships, my work, and my life. We are all in a continual process of evolution. During those moments when I forget or I am not aware that I am no longer embodying these agreements, I ask that others speak that truth to me with compassion and I will do the same for them.

# Community Agreements

Heartwood Cohousing is a rural cohousing community founded in 1999. Made up of people of all ages and from all walks of life, these Agreements have been at the core of communications for the twenty-four households. Gail, a founding resident, says, "The Agreements are the foundation and the reason our community is thriving." For Gail's whole story, go to http://www.revolutionarychoices.com/results.

The following is taken verbatim from the website of the Heartwood CoHousing Community.

## INTERPERSONAL AGREEMENTS (01/07/99)

**To Communicate With Integrity**
I agree to tell my truth, with compassion for myself and others, and to trust that others are doing the same.

**To Listen With My Heart**
I agree to listen respectfully to the communications of others and attune to their deepest meaning.

**To Own My Feelings**
I agree to take responsibility for my feelings and how I react to the words and actions of others. And I agree to express those feelings in a spirit of openness and compassion.

**To Honor Each Person's Process**
I agree to acknowledge that everyone, including myself, is making the best possible choice or decision we are capable of at that moment.

**To Express Appreciation**
I agree to appreciate others and myself.

### To Cooperate with Others
I agree to maintain a sense of cooperation and caring in my interactions with others.

### To Honor Our Differences
I understand that goals are often the same even though methods for achieving them may differ.

### To Be Aware of Conflict
I agree to look for the unresolved issues within me that create a disproportionate adverse reaction to another's behavior.

### To Resolve Conflicts Constructively
I agree to take problems and complaints to the person(s) with whom I can resolve them, at the earliest opportunity. I agree not to criticize or complain to someone who cannot do something about my complaint, and I will redirect others to do the same. I will not say behind someone's back what I am not willing to say to their face.

### To Maintain Harmony
I agree to take the time to establish rapport with others and then to reconnect with anyone with whom I feel out of harmony as soon as it is appropriate.

### To Freely Participate
I agree to freely choose and re-choose to participate in the Heartwood Cohousing Community. It is my choice.

### To Lighten Up!
I agree to allow fun and joy in my relationships, my work, and my life.

(Note: These Interpersonal Agreements are based in large part on those of Geneva Community.)

## Core Groups around the Globe

In 1988, UN NGO Global Family Founder Carolyn Anderson and Trained Facilitator Tim Claus expanded the Geneva Group Agreements into what they dubbed The Co-Creator's Agreements. Global Family's Hummingbird Community adapted them further. They continue to evolve as community members and the hundreds of small core groups seeded by Global Family worldwide evolve. To learn more, visit http://www.globalfamily.net and http://www .hummingbirdcommunity.org/.

These Agreements are published in *The Co-Creator's Handbook: An Experiential Guide for Discovering Your Life's Purpose* and in a variety of publications by Carolyn Anderson.

## Be Mindful
My intent is to be myself, to be authentic, and to be fully present.

## Realize our Potential
My commitment is to realize my full potential and support others in doing the same.

## Follow my Guidance
I agree to attune with spirit and follow the calling of my soul on behalf of the well-being of the whole.

## Communicate with Integrity
I agree to tell my truth with compassion for myself and others.

## Act with Integrity
I agree to keep my agreements and will do my best to follow my heart in making commitments.

## Deep Listening
I agree to listen respectfully to the communication of others and tune in to their deepest meaning.

## Honor One Another
I agree to honor each person's process, acknowledging that everyone, including myself, is making the best possible choice or decision we are capable of in that moment.

## Appreciate Our Contributions
I agree to acknowledge others for their contributions to the good of the whole.

## Honor Our Differences
I agree to come from a sense of cooperation and caring in my inter-actions with others, and from an understanding that objectives are

often the same even though methods for achieving them may differ. I honor the diversity of all life.

## Take Responsibility

I agree to take responsibility for my creations, my reactions, my experience, and my relationships.

## Maintain Resonance

I agree to take the time to establish rapport and then to reconnect with anyone with whom I feel out of harmony as soon as it may be appropriate.

## Resolve Problems Constructively

I agree to offer at least one solution any time I present a problem. I agree to take problems, complaints, and upsets to the person(s) with whom I can resolve them, at the earliest opportunity. I agree not to criticize or complain to someone who cannot do something about my complaint, and I will redirect others to do the same.

## Go for Excellence

I agree to support others and to be supported in participating at the highest level of excellence.

## Learn from Experience

I agree to do my best to learn from my experiences.

## Accept Imperfections

I intend to embrace and accept the imperfections of myself and others.

## Be a Leader

I agree to foster an environment of genuine collaboration, in which all people, including myself, feel empowered to express our individual and collective potential.

## Service to Others

I am willing to open my heart, still my mind, and be in compassionate service to all life.

## Re-evaluate My Commitment

I agree to choose and re-choose to participate in this community. It is my choice.

**Lighten Up**

While honoring all these agreements and taking them seriously, I aspire to do so with an attitude of light-heartedness.

# Agreements for the Executive Branch

In 1992, my husband, Glenn, and I were invited to submit our process for team cohesion to the White House transition team preparing for the start of a new administration. The following is excerpted from *The American Team: 7 Steps to Genuine Teamwork in the White House and Beyond.*

1. **Commit to the Mission:**
   I agree to support the mission of my organization and to use it as a guide to my actions.

2. **Communicate with Integrity:**
   I agree to be honest, thorough, and responsible in my communications.

3. **Listen Openly:**
   I agree to listen respectfully to the communications of others and to be receptive to the meaning behind the words.

4. **Honor One Another:**
   I agree to acknowledge that everyone, including myself, is making the best possible choice or decision we are capable of at that moment of choice or decision.

5. **Appreciate Our Own Contributions:**
   I agree to take responsibility for acknowledging myself and receiving acknowledgment from others.

6. **Express Appreciation for Others' Contributions:**
   I agree to acknowledge others.

7. **Honor Differences:**
   I agree to operate from a sense of cooperation and caring in my interactions with others, understanding that goals are often the same even though methods for achieving them may differ.

8. **Use Grievances as Opportunities for Growth:**
   I agree to look for unresolved issues within me that create disproportionate reactions to others' behavior.

9. **Resolve Problems Constructively:**
   I agree to offer at least one solution any time I present a problem. I agree to take problems, complaints, and upsets to the person(s) with whom I can resolve them, at the earliest opportunity. I agree not to criticize or complain to someone who cannot do something about my complaint, and I will redirect others to do the same.

10. **Go For Excellence!**
    I agree to support others and to be supported in participating at the highest levels of excellence.

11. **Learn From Experience:**
    I agree to look for opportunities to learn from my experiences, to continue doing what works and discontinue doing what does not work.

12. **Be a Leader:**
    I agree to foster an environment of genuine collaboration, in which all people, including myself, feel empowered to express our individual and collective potential.

13. **Re-evaluate Our Commitment:**
    I agree to choose and re-choose to participate in this organization. It's my choice!

14. **Lighten Up!**
    I agree to create joy in my relationships, my work, and my life.

# $\mathcal{N}$OTES

## Why This Second Edition?

1  If you'd like to read the complete collection of stories shared by our readers, you can do so online at http://revolutionarychoices.com/results/ and in archived issues of Revolutionary News, where most stories were originally published, at http://revolutionaryagreements.com/news.html.

2  William J. Long, "Quantum Theory and Neuroplasticity: Implications for Social Theory," *Journal of Theoretical and Philosophical Psychology* 26, nos.1-2 (2006): 78-94. http://dx.doi.org/10.1037/h0091268; http://www .collective-evolution.com/2014/03/08/10-scientific-studies-that-prove-consciousness-can-alter-our-physical-material-world/.

3  http://revolutionarychoices.com/easy/.

4  David R. Hawkins, *Power vs. Force* (Carlsbad: Hay House, 2014). To read my published review of *Power vs. Force* for Amazon, go to: https://goo.gl/R9Yu5a.
   Two elucidating commentaries can be found at: http://nancy-bragin.com/2012/12/29/dr-david-hawkins-calibrated-reading-list/and http://www.stevepavlina.com/blog/2005/04 /levels-of-consciousness/.

## Birth of the Revolutionary Agreements

1  The personal development program that inspired the Geneva Group Agreements, which later evolved into the Revolutionary

Agreements, is "Money and You: Management by Agreement."
I am grateful to Marshall Thurber for his brilliant design and
expert facilitation of this life-changing program. Thurber was
founder of the enormously successful Hawthorne/Stone Real
Estate Company of San Francisco, written about in *New
Realities* magazine (Brown 1977). According to Laurie Weiss
in *What is the Emperor Wearing? Truth-Telling in Business
Relationships,* "The Hawthorne/Stone agreements are reputed
to have been created as 'rules of the game' in a business that
was introducing the radical (in the mid 1970s) concept of
using principles of the heart in a business environment. The
agreements were said to be ideas that were tested by the working
group to see what impact they would have on the productivity
and personal growth of the people involved. Those principles
that had a positive effect were retained; the others were dis-
carded." My special thanks to Laurie Weiss and her husband,
Jon, for producing the "Money and You" program in Colorado,
where I was introduced to "Rules of the Game." Marshall
Thurber continues to offer transformational programs through
http://www.burklynglobal.com. To learn about current
"Money and You" programs, go to http://www.excellerated.com.

[2] Named Geneva Group, this forum was founded June 8, 1985,
at the home of Glenn and Marian Head and Gail Hoag in
Geneva Park, Boulder, Colorado. We owe a debt of gratitude
to the founding members (in addition to Glenn, Gail, and
myself): Lycia Adams, Don Darling, Thomas Duncan, John
Erhard, Dale and Dar Emme, Sigrid Farwell, Susan O'Neil,
Sharon Proudfit, Lindsay Robinson, Donne Ruiz, Diane
Schmitz, Liz Gardener, and Carol Ann Wilson Fullmer. We are
deeply grateful to Carol Hoskins for keeping the forum alive
and well during Glenn's and my early parenting years.
We are also deeply grateful to those who later joined with
founding members, creating a core that continued to meet
monthly for twenty years to fulfill this purpose: *The Geneva*

*Group is an ever growing union of individuals who acknowledge, accept, and manifest the love of higher consciousness that guides us to create a model for a harmonious world.*

The mission of Geneva Group, revealed to participants in 1985, remains intact today: *Geneva Group is an energy storehouse similar to a battery; people from all over the world connect to it, bringing their skills, knowledge, energy, and vision. We are committed to allowing the Divine Being in us to manifest through us in this storage center where we get charged and recharge others. Our mission is to develop and maximize our personal growth and evolution, thus enhancing our relationships and all life on the planet through reflecting unconditional love, support, growth, and well-being. We joyfully acknowledge that we are the whole, bonded through the God spirit residing within each of us.*

<sup>3</sup> The Soviet-American Citizens' Summits mentioned here and discussed throughout this book were created and produced by Rama Joyti Vernon and Barbara Marx Hubbard, alongside their Soviet counterparts from the Soviet Peace Committee and other state-authorized agencies.

Rama is Founding President of the Center for International Dialogue (formerly Center for Soviet-American Dialogue), Founder and President Emeritus of Women of Vision and Action (WOVA), cofounder of the *Yoga Journal*, and citizen-diplomat for conflict resolution dialogues worldwide. Mikhail Gorbachev credited her citizen diplomacy efforts as a major contribution to ending Cold War stereotypes.

Barbara Marx Hubbard (http://barbaramarxhubbard.com/) is President of the Foundation for Conscious Evolution, founding member of the World Future Society, an internationally recognized speaker, and the prolific author of many books including *Conscious Evolution: Awakening the Power of our Social Potential, Emergence, 52 Codes for Conscious Self Evolution*, and (along with myself) *The Suprasexual rEvolution*. Additionally, Barbara produced the award-winning

*Humanity Ascending* series of DVDs. Barbara's work focuses on providing processes and tools (including forms of the Revolutionary Agreements) through which the vast global movement for positive change can align, connect, and further cooperate toward the common goal of a compassionate, sustainable future that recognizes and supports the interconnectedness of all life. Barbara was one of the first women to have her name placed in nomination for Vice President of the United States (at the 1984 Democratic National Convention).

An inspiring and informative book documents the vision and results of the first Soviet-American Citizens' Summit: *Citizen Diplomacy Progress Report 1989: The USSR*, edited by Sandy McCune Jeffrey (now Sandy Westin) (Boulder: Clearinghouse for Citizen Diplomacy, 1989). In addition to documenting the hundreds of projects jointly initiated during that first auspicious convening in Washington, DC, the book includes essays on citizen diplomacy by Rama Vernon, Barbara Marx Hubbard, members of the Soviet Peace Committee, and others that shine the light on this epochal moment in history.

Following is an excerpt from pages 46–47, reprinted with permission of the editor, which was written by Summit collaborator Andre Nuikin, then Senior Researcher at the Institute of Arts Studies of the USSR Ministry of Culture:

*It is impossible to approach this diplomacy with old yardsticks, demanding perceptible results, well-planned stages, constructive forms. This is not a mechanical increase of uniting structures that is taking place here, but an alchemy of souls, the sacrament of the birth of a living being from the effect of Aladdin's lamp. The main argument in this diplomacy is not the number of warheads, not the productivity of blast furnaces, nor the figures of commodity circulation, but the expression in the eyes of people who meet one another, the strength of handshakes, goodwill, and the wit of jokes. Therefore we must meet, talk, touch one another, and smile, although for political and scientific general-*

*izations, all this material is purely ephemeral and beyond all calculation.*

*"Beauty will save the world!" proclaimed Fyodor Dostoyevsky. Indeed, it is precisely beauty that will save the world. Not museum beauty, of course, but that which looks for an outlet (but so far finds it so rarely) in our souls. No, not just any kind of beauty will save us; the flight of a missile with nuclear warheads too may be seen as beautiful. Our salvation is in the beauty of human relations—generosity, conscience, friendliness, trust, and high intellect. By "high" I mean the intellect which is not separated from the beauty of spiritual movements, does not contradict them but is blended with them indissolubly. Here we also have to revise the yardsticks and standards.*

*Spirituality today is, I would say, sympathy for the world which has attained a scope of all mankind. To be spiritual means to have an open heart for all global problems of the century, to take to heart all troubles of one's people and mankind, to rejoice at their joys, to be personally responsible for the past, the present, and the future.*

For reprints of selected sections of Citizen Diplomacy, contact the editor, Sandy Westin, swestin@villageassistance.com.

4   In October 1985, ten spiritual leaders (two each from five major religions) and eight elected officials from parliaments on five continents met in Tarrytown, New York, to explore the possibility of a dialogue intermingling their perspectives. As a result, the Global Forum of Spiritual and Parliamentary Leaders on Human Survival was born. Alongside our colleagues from Global Family, a UN Non-Governmental Organization (NGO), Glenn and I were honored to collaborate on the design and implementation of the first Global Forums. In April 1988, under the coordination of Akio Matsumura, a Global Survival Conference brought nearly 200 spiritual and legislative leaders to the historic university city of Oxford, England. For five days, parliamentarians and cabinet members met with cardinals,

swamis, bishops, rabbis, imams, monks, and elders. Among them were H.H. the Dalai Lama, Mother Teresa, the Archbishop of Canterbury, and Native American spiritual leader Chief Oren Lyons. These leaders conferred with experts on the issues, including astronomer Carl Sagan, Soviet scientist Evgeny Velikhov, Gaia scientist James Lovelock, Kenyan environmental leader Wangari Maathai, and Cosmonaut Valentina Tereshkova.

In the end, the vision a few had worked for became a shared vision among many. Spiritual and parliamentary leaders from fifty-two countries, along with participating scientists and influential journalists, left Oxford agreeing that "we both need and desire to work together" to protect Earth and all that lives on it. Future Forums in Moscow, Rio de Janeiro, and Kyoto served to solidify relationships and strategies for implementation.

[5] Marian Head and Glenn Head, *The American Team: 7 Steps to Genuine Teamwork in the White House and Beyond* (Boulder: New World Design Center, 1992). This was prepared and submitted by invitation to the Clinton/Gore Presidential transition team and subsequently incorporated into *Blueprint for Presidential Transition* (Washington, DC, 1992).

[6] Laurie Weiss, *What Is the Emperor Wearing? Truth-Telling in Business Relationships* (Boston: Butterworth-Heinemann, 1998).

[7] Brian Brook, *Love Styles: Re-Engineering Marriage for the New Millennium* (Denver: ProSe, 2000).

[8] Carolyn Anderson with Katharine Roske, *The Co-Creator's Handbook: An Experiential Guide for Discovering Your Life's Purpose and Building a Co-Creative Society* (Global Family, 2015). *The Co-Creator's Handbook* is a source book for all those who choose to co-create a positive future for our world by shifting consciousness from separation and fear to unity and love. Global Family promotes activities, processes, and

practices that enable people to experience deeper connections to each other, to the earth, and to their Source. Global Family promotes changing social structures from a model of domination to a partnership model. *The Co-Creator's Handbook* includes The Co-Creator's Agreements, an early version of the Revolutionary Agreements (http://www.globalfamily.net).

9  Martie McMane, *Living Grace: Spiritual Growth in the Everyday World* (Boulder: Marlin Press, 2011).

## The One Agreement

1  In *Essential Spirituality: The 7 Central Practices to Awaken Heart and Mind* (New York: John Wiley & Sons, 2000), Roger Walsh, MD, PhD, beautifully summarizes the essential message of the seven great world religions in this way: Judaism: He is in all, and all is in Him. Christianity: The Kingdom of Heaven is within you. Islam: Those who know themselves know their Lord. Confucianism: Those who know completely their own nature, know heaven. Chinese Book of Changes: In the depth of the soul, one sees the Divine, the One. Hinduism: Individual consciousness and universal consciousness are one. Buddhism: Look within, you are the Buddha.

2  Don Miguel Ruiz, *The Four Agreements: A Practical Guide to Personal Freedom* (San Rafael, CA: Amber-Allen Publishing, 1997).

## I agree to live my mission.

1  Anderson and Roske, *The Co-Creator's Handbook*.

2  Po Bronson, *What Should I Do With My Life? The True Story of People Who Answered the Ultimate Question* (New York: Random House, 2003).

3  Stephen Covey, *The 7 Habits of Highly Successful People: Powerful Lessons in Personal Change* (New York: Simon & Schuster, 1990).

4  Stephen Covey, A. Roger Merrill, and Rebecca R. Merrill, *First Things First: To Live, To Love, To Learn, To Leave a Legacy* (New York: Fireside, 1996).

5  Michael Gerber, *The E-Myth Revisited: Why Most Small Businesses Don't Work and What to Do About It* (New York: Harper Business, 1995), 190–209.

6  McMane, *Living Grace*, 5.

7  Marc Lesser, *Less: Accomplishing More by Doing Less* (Novato, CA: New World Library, 2009), 5-8.

## I agree to speak my truth, with compassion.

1  http://abcnews.go.com/US/united-airlines-officials-highlight-misses-safety-message-pilots/story?id=29237744.

2  The team of astronauts aboard the spaceship Columbia were described by Gary Dorsey in *The Baltimore Sun*, February 7, 2003.

## I agree to look within when I react.

1  McMane, *Living Grace*, 53-54.

2  Ruiz, *The Four Agreements*, 48-49.

## I agree to keep doing what works and change what doesn't.

1  Dianne Collins, *Do You QuantumThink? New Thinking That Will Rock Your World* (New York: Select Books, 2011). This author and her husband, Alan Collins, who served magnificently as Glenn's and my business team's QuantumThink® coach for three years, have influenced significantly the way we think. Dianne and I envision joining forces to offer Quantum-Thinking and the Revolutionary Agreements to our US Congress to help them to move forward with the updated thinking needed to address pressing issues of our times.

2 Kathryn McCamant, *Cohousing: A Contemporary Approach to Housing Ourselves, 2nd Edition* (Berkeley: Ten Speed Press, 1993). This book and its author guided us and many thousands of others on our community building journey.

3 Not being a TV watcher, I didn't know at the time that the "EASY" button was sold at Staples and shown on many Staples commercials.

## I agree to listen with my heart.

1 I have learned a great deal about myself and the filters through which I listen from Carol McCall's "Empowerment of Listening" seminars. McCall is founder of the Institute for Global Listening and Communication (http://www.listeningprofitsu .com) and author of *Listen! There's a World Waiting To Be Heard* (New York: Vantage Press, 2000).

2 Peter Senge. *Fifth Discipline Fieldbook: Strategies and Tools for Building a Learning Organization* (New York: Crown Business, 1994), 377.

## I agree to respect our differences.

1 Susan Cain. *Quiet: The Power of Introverts in a World that Can't Stop Talking* (New York: Broadway Books, 2012).

2 McMane, *Living Grace*, 90-91.

## I agree to resolve conflicts directly.

1 For a fuller description of how two monogamous couples shared a home together for nearly thirteen years, read Brian Brook's *Love Styles: Re-Engineering Marriage for the New Millennium.*

## I agree to honor our choices.

[1] http://goo.gl/dgtuV0

[2] McMane, *Living Grace*, 29.

[3] Covey, *The 7 Habits of Highly Effective People*, 90.

[4] Collins, *Do You QuantumThink?*, 167-168.

[5] From http://www.hooponopono.org.

## I agree to give and receive thanks.

[1] This oft-quoted passage appears to be expanded from the following, which appeared in an interview in a 1989 edition of *Time* magazine: "The hunger for love is much more difficult to remove than the hunger for bread."

[2] Marian Head, *Gratitude Journal for a Healthy Marriage* (Boulder: Marlin Press, 2015). Available for purchase online at www.gratitudejournalnow.com.

[3] http://www.health.harvard.edu/newsletter_article/in-praise-of-gratitude.

[4] On CBS TV, December 30, 1957. The full quotation is: "No matter how big a nation is, it is not stronger than its weakest people, and as long as you keep a person down, some part of you has to be down there to hold him down, so it means that you cannot soar as you might otherwise."

[5] McMane, *Living Grace*, 132.

[6] Alfie Kohn, *Punished by Rewards: The Trouble with Gold Stars, Incentive Plans, A's, Praise, and Other Bribes* (New York: Mariner Books, 1999).

## I agree to look for blessings in disguise.

[1] I met David Kimmel in an exceptional spiritual development program developed by Arjuna Ardagh. David was one of the

program's facilitators. He personally helped me through several deep issues that took a lifetime to accumulate and days to dissolve. Years later, when faced with mounting uncontrollable emotions around my son's illness, I thought of Arjuna's process and David's ability to help me relax into the vastness of love. I have lost contact with David but not with Arjuna, who continues to teach his amazing process to other coaches. I recently had an excellent experience with one of those coaches, Sharon Mauldin. You can "Find A Coach" at http://www .awakeningcoachingtraining.com.

[2] Lin Yutang, *The Importance of Living* (New York: William Morrow Paperbacks, 1998). (Originally published in 1937.)

## I agree to lighten up!

[1] From the website of the Association for Applied and Therapeutic Humor, http://www.AATH.org.

[2] Norman Cousins, *Anatomy of an Illness: As perceived by the patient* (New York: W. W. Norton & Company, 2005).

[3] McMane, *Living Grace*, 119.

## Creating a Positive World

[1] *The Revolutionary Agreements Facilitator's Guide* may be downloaded for free from the store at http://www .revolutionarychoices.com.

[2] Malcolm Gladwell, *The Tipping Point: How Little Things Can Make a Big Difference* (New York: Little Brown and Company, 2000).

[3] Reprinted by permission by Sevanne Kassarjian from The Institute for Intercultural Studies in New York, founded by Margaret Mead in 1944. Explained on their web page, http://www.interculturalstudies.org/faq.html#quote: "Although the Institute has received many inquiries about this

famous admonition by Margaret Mead, we have been unable to locate when and where it was first cited, becoming a motto for many organizations and movements. We believe it probably came into circulation through a newspaper report of something said spontaneously and informally. We know, however, that it was firmly rooted in her professional work and that it reflected a conviction that she expressed often, in different contexts and phrasings."

# $\mathcal{A}$BOUT THE AUTHOR

Marian Head has been initiating revolutions in business, government, and education since the early 1970s.

Her diverse experiences as an organizer, facilitator, entrepreneur, and leader began when she was the child-President of her 4-H Club and have traversed a variety of venues since, including: first Manager for Educational Development at the US Senate; top 100 sales leader for seven consecutive years at a global nutrition company; cochair of a graduate school department of Leadership and Organizational Transformation; founder of Marlin Press and its "Professional Trainers' Collection"; program coordinator for historic Soviet-American Citizens' Summits in Washington, DC and Moscow; and co-facilitator of the first two Global Forums of Spiritual and Parliamentary Leaders in Oxford and Moscow.

In 1985, alongside her husband, Glenn, Marian cofounded the Geneva Group, a network of businesspeople formed around a set of principles that subsequently evolved into the Revolutionary Agreements. Marian has devoted herself to introducing these principles into the lives and work of hundreds of thousands of people worldwide.

Marian's passion for the principles of authentic leadership and compassionate communication have led her to speak to audiences of thousands, consult with organizations ranging from small businesses to Fortune 100 corporations, serve on and chair national and international committees and boards for both profit and nonprofit organizations, and continually explore new ways to fulfill her passion to be of service to humanity.

Marian is the award-winning author of *Revolutionary Agreements: Twelve Ways to Transform Stress and Struggle Into Freedom and Joy* (2005) and *Gratitude Journal for a Healthy Marriage* (2015). She coauthored with Barbara Marx Hubbard *The Suprasexual rEvolution* (2012).

Marlin Press is dedicated to providing publications
and presentations that make a positive difference
in the life of each person we touch.

To order books and posters,
visit the online store at:
**www.revolutionarychoices.com**

Special discounts on bulk quantities are available
to businesses, non-profit organizations, congregations,
book clubs, and study groups. Contact us at:
**www.revolutionarychoices.com/contact**

To contact the author about keynote workshops or coaching,
please send an email to:
**marian@revolutionaryagreements.com**

To learn how to become a
Certified Revolutionary Agreements Coach, visit:
**www.agreementsinstitute.com**